W9-ABG-812

THE STORY OF THE NOVEL

PN
3491
.W3
1979

THE STORY OF THE NOVEL

GEORGE WATSON

BOOKS

10 East 53d St., New York 10022
(a division of Harper & Row Publishers, Inc.)

WITHDRAWN

Salem Academy and College
Gramley Library
Winston-Salem, N.C. 27108

© George Watson 1979

All rights reserved. No part of this publication
may be reproduced or transmitted, in any form
or by any means, without permission.

First published in Great Britain 1979 by
The Macmillan Press Ltd

Published in the U.S.A. 1979 by
HARPER & ROW PUBLISHERS, INC.
BARNES AND NOBLE IMPORT DIVISION

Printed in Great Britain

Library of Congress Cataloging in Publication Data

Watson, George, 1927–
  The story of the novel.

  Bibliography: p.
  Includes index.
    1. Fiction—History and criticism.   2. Fiction—
Technique.   I. Title.
PN3491.W3   1979   809.3′3   79–13093
ISBN 0–06–497493–6
ISBN 0–06–497494–4   pbk.

Contents

FOR
VIVIENNE MYLNE

Acknowledgements

This book started life as a series of lectures for undergraduates reading English at Cambridge, and has profited in more ways I can easily count from their questioning attention. It was the lack of any book appropriate to student needs that first stirred me to this attempt.

Most of the works (I cannot seriously hope all) to which I feel indebted in argument are listed in an appendix as 'Notes for Further Reading'. I hope this arrangement will look more useful than a series of interruptions to my own text, and none the less grateful.

In the course of writing I have grown variously indebted for advice, most often to Cambridge friends and colleagues such as Elsie Duncan-Jones, Michael Beddow, Patrick Boyde, Peter Croft and Colin Smith, as well as to P. G. Boucé of Paris and Robert A. Day of New York. And to my dedicatee, Vivienne Mylne of the University of Kent at Canterbury, I owe the rewards of twenty years of talk about European fiction, and an irreverent eye for exposing some general law that an individual case has obstinately failed to observe.

St John's College, Cambridge   G.W.
September 1978

Preface

A story is the best thing about a novel. But the title of this book, which is deliberately ambiguous, is meant to suggest something more than that. 'Novel' is the name of a literary kind, and there is a story to tell about how, over the centuries, its substance has widened and its conventions changed. This book is about both: it is at once a study of nrrative, and a history of the novel since its emergence some three centuries ago.

Its pattern differs, however, from older histories like Ernest Baker's or Walter Allen's, which moved chronologically from novelist to novelist. In this book I shall move rather from one aspect of narrative to another, though some chapters are broadly historical within themselves. Since no two readers have read the same novels, the best way to use it might be as a framework: a sort of clothes-horse to hang one's own instances on – relating what one has read, or means to read, to the outline offered here.

Critical debate suggests that the study of fiction now needs just that. The problem of narrative by now represents a highly sophisticated inquiry – so much so that it is sometimes hard to find one's way back to the starting-point, or to get at the facts that a reader of fiction now needs in order to acquire a sense of what is exceptional and what is ordinary. That is because it is always a temptation for critics to write with the object of impressing other critics: and one worth resisting, if hard to resist. My first impulse was to write an elementary book rather than an original one; though originality sometimes comes unlooked for, and elementary arguments have a way of turning irresistibly into something else. And any working historian knows that it is easier to be original than to get it right.

Henry James, in an excited moment, called the novel 'independent, elastic, prodigious', and its story is as untidy as some of its masterpieces. It is already hard to achieve a 'poetic' of it, or working handbook, and it will doubtless get harder. If Aristotle had ever read any novels, he would have needed a far wider canvas than he allowed to tragedy in that surviving fragment of analysis known as the *Poetics*. My own view is that the novel none the less calls for analysis in something like the Aristotelian style, even though it now amounts to some three centuries of endeavour in all the great literary languages of the Western world. By Aristotelian here I mean a tradition which is analytically concerned with formal elements considered as ways of representing realities, or as mimetic devices; and one hospitable to historical reference, too, since those devices change from age to age. The study now needs a sense of form that is not merely formalistic. All that could help in contemporary judgement too. Twentieth-century novels are powerfully reminiscent of their origins, to an informed eye, and especially of that highly formative century between Defoe and Scott, Lesage and Balzac.

It is in this spirit that I am concerned here with form: as a complex of devices for representing reality. That is why I have devoted a first chapter to the defence of realism: a doctrine that dogmatically upholds the claims of fiction to represent the real, and in my view fundamentally right. All that has meant shifting the argument from single novels or novelists towards a sense of how novels relate to one another in long ancestral lines. The sympathetic reader will have to expect to shift his interests in a similar direction. It is one thing to read novels, as most of us do; another to reflect efficiently about the novel as an evolving literary kind, much though the one activity depends upon the other. In that sense, this book is about the Novel rather than novels. It considers how a great literary species was moulded into a recognisable life of its own, and how its conventions have evolved since the seventeenth century.

A European community existed in fiction before statesmen were inspired and encouraged to make institutions of it, and no boundaries of nation or period can reasonably limit this inquiry, though my main emphasis falls on novels composed in English and in French. The twentieth century, as I see it, has been rich above all in its faculty to revive and adapt, and many of its experiments are best seen as reflections of preceding ages. That reminder could be salutary: one odd effect of the cult of the New since the 1950s has been to exalt as original some narrative practices that Diderot or Sterne would have found unsurprising; and some fashionable arguments about meta-fictionality strike me as ignorant, and perhaps wilfully ignorant at that.

The *nouveau roman* of the 1960s was nothing like as *nouveau* as its name suggested. Post-war fiction has plenty of lively and original elements to boast of; but seeing what is original calls for some widely shared knowledge of the sources out of which modern techniques have grown. That is the first object of this book.

By and large, and with that object in mind, I have concerned myself with novels that are famous, or at least known; and some of my assertions about the primacy of events may seem over-bold and omissive unless seen in the light of that guiding principle. To deal largely with known books is a matter of courtesy, in the first instance, since any reader would prefer to hear about novels which he has read, or may soon read. It is also more useful. And it is compelled upon the historian, in any case, by a body of evidence so vast that his own knowledge is necessarily partial and imperfect. But masterpieces cannot be grasped in isolation, and my scope is rather wider than that. Great art, as F. Scott Fitzgerald once remarked in his notes, 'is the contempt of a great man for small art', and to feel that contempt one needs to know something about small art, and to widen one's interests beyond the best. If it has proved difficult to maintain a balance in this delicate matter, I hope that the general principle, at least, can be conceded.

1 *An Apology for Fiction*

A defence, or 'apologie', for fiction in the present age must mean one that upholds its claim to describe the real. That defence, by now, is inescapable. The descriptive claim is at once under heavy attack, and yet fundamental to the classic pretensions of the novel over three centuries. That is because the great novelists of the European past have claimed to describe, and even to describe accurately, and we do them little honour in praising them for having achieved something else. And since realism is by now the most familiar name for the descriptive claims of fiction, this argument will turn irresistibly into its defence, though it will run wider than the works of the great nineteenth-century realists.

To practise realism, it is often argued, or to defend its theoretical claims, now belongs to a tradition that is quaintly antique and obstinately British. British novelists since the Second World War have somehow acquired a reputation for hostility to experiment and for a cosy, naïve assumption that novels are after all concerned with social accuracy. My own view is that the case for realism is better than this orthodox view allows us to see; that the argument about nationality has been misconceived; and that realism, far from being antique, is more modern than its rivals.

If experiment here means a playful awareness of fictional technique on the part of the novelist, or 'fictionality', then the British enjoyed their experimental period earlier than the French or the Americans. Fictions that exploit some logical absurdity in narrative existed in English at least as early as Sterne's *Tristram Shandy* in the mid-eighteenth century, or Robert Southey's narrative medley *The Doctor* early in the nineteenth. A sense of the 'fictive' in fiction is very far from recent in the English novel: a fact that may help to explain why much that looks *nouveau* in Paris looks old-hat in London.

Nor has English fiction simply abandoned its fictive interests in favour of realism. On the contrary, the two have run sidelong and interweaving courses, where priorities are difficult to establish. Richardson, Fielding and Smollett published before Sterne, who parodies their descriptive pretensions; and Dickens, Thackeray and Trollope do not exclude fictive devices when they write realistic novels. Fictionality, being familiar to Rabelais and Cervantes, is older than Sterne, and it never died between *Don Quixote* and the French *nouveau roman*. In the present century, as early as 1925, André Gide wrote *Les Faux-monnayeurs*, a novel in which a novelist is writing a novel . . . ; so that fictive devices are not recent in French either, in this century, as deliberated forms, and they have a long if intermittent tradition in both languages. James Joyce was not an isolated phenomenon between the wars. Samuel Beckett's *Murphy* appeared in 1938. And in 1939, the same year as Joyce's *Finnegans Wake*, 'Flann O'Brien' (or Brian O'Nolan) produced *At Swim-Two-Birds*, a novel narrated by an Irish student writing a novel about a certain Trellis, who is writing a book about his enemies; they, in revenge, are writing one about Trellis. . . . And in 1962 Doris Lessing's *Golden Notebook* appeared: a long study by a novelist unable to write a novel, as commonly understood though still capable of setting out her convictions, and confusions, about the state of mankind.

★

The real case against realism, however, is an argument about narrative.

The anti-realist, who by now is easily recognised by his habit of calling novels 'texts' and by an obsession with the fictive, may have been the source and origin of a good deal of nonsense, but he has undeniably performed two services to be thankful for. The first is to have drawn attention away from style and towards story. He has returned narrative, and rightly, to the centre of argument. The rewards of that new attention may still be something less than clear, but that is a deficiency that may be repaired with time. I take it that story in fiction, like melody in music, is at once fundamental, and fundamentally baffling. There is still no general theory that accounts for its potency, and no general system to which instances can be efficiently related. Quest or pursuit, love requital, or what V. S. Pritchett once memorably called the Principle of Procrastinated Rape – all this does not yet amount to an effective taxonomy of the subject. And yet, whatever the difficulties, it cannot be acceptable simply to leave story out. The French New Critics of the 1960s may have been rash in rejecting the claims of realism, and inconclusive in their attempts to create a general theory of narrative. But at least they could see that story matters. We can all stop apologising for it.

The second, and consequent, service has been to restore an interest in form: the conventions by which novelists shape the stories they have to tell. That interest is not new. Form was the grand, echoing obsession of Henry James's New York prefaces of 1907–9, written in his mid-sixties for a revised collection of his novels. It was a brisk launching, but the half century that followed showed little progress in the question. Perhaps it was felt that James's own tentative solutions to formal problems were too intimately inbound with his own fictions – fictions of a highly analytical kind that novelists in the 1920s and 1930s were no longer even trying to write.

More recent formalism, at all events, has not been Jamesian. As it re-emerged in the 1950s, mainly in French and Anglo-American criticism, it was the work of academics rather than of novelists, and it arose out of a post-war fashion for structural linguistics. Structuralism was a doctrine of patterns within language and, more recently, in anthropology and literature, based on a concept of symmetries of which binary opposition was the simplest. It has proved a poor exchange, however, for the rich suggestive impulses of James's essays. For one thing, a novel is too untidy an object, often, to be seen as regulated in its entirety, and the patterns offered can be impoverishing: the figure in the carpet is not itself the carpet, or anything like it. For another, the lineage of fiction needs to be studied with some sense of historical chronology: it is one thing to write a letter-novel in the late eighteenth century, when the form was in vogue – quite another to attempt it in the late twentieth. And again, a novel is a fund of knowledge as well as a literary form; and any pure and exclusive formalism, whether structuralist or other, flies in the face of much of the ordinary experience of reading fiction. People still read novels, thank goodness, but many critics now read texts. That is parody, but a parody with too much truth for comfort. To the extent that it is true, it poses an odd problem. The need now is less to turn people into critics than critics into people.

My present task is to construct an historical diagram of the novel over three centuries that will work as a frame of reference, enabling the reader to relate what he knows of novels, or may some day know, to a sense of how forms were created, and how they evolved.

★

The knowledge that fiction offers is of life itself. It would hardly be worth bothering with otherwise.

> Were there not a matter known,
> There would be no passion,

as Herrick once put it; and the novel has undeniably excited passion – whether anxiety, detestation or love. 'As a people, the novel is educating us',[1] an American poet told a Baltimore audience in 1881, holding up to view a copy of James's recent novel *The American* which he had borrowed from a local library, and which already bore on its covers the signs of wear. Novels can inform on some surprising subjects, what is more, such as the naval expedition to Carthagena in Smollett's *Roderick Random*, or the Highland revolt of 1745 in Scott's *Waverley*, or Napoleon's invasion of Russia in Tolstoy's *War and Peace*; or more general truths, as Melville in *Moby Dick* informs us about the corrosive human obsession with evil as well as the mating habits of the sperm whale. Proust tells us about social manners in the Belle Epoque, C. P. Snow about how Britain was administered in the 1940s and 1950s, and Defoe's *Robinson Crusoe* about what to do with things on, and by implication off, a desert island; and there are novels that will tell you how to cook a meal, or win a lover or an argument. Like other kinds of story, a novel is a way of learning about how things were or are – cognitive instrument; and those who distrust stories as evidence should consider how often in conversation we use them to make points or answer questions. 'In our lives we are always weaving novels', as Trollope aptly remarks in his *Autobiography* (1883) (ch. 9). A question in conversation like 'Is he reliable?' might well be answered: 'The last time he made an appointment with me, he never turned up, and he didn't even say he was sorry.' That is to tell a story, and a story more informative than the answer 'Yes' or 'No' would be.

Stories, whether true or fictional, instruct; and readers of novels over three centuries are very unlikely to have been wrong in thinking they were learning about life as they read them. Professional critics who deny all that are merely labouring to disprove the obvious. Indeed the novel is so convincing an account of life that it even possesses the sinister power of misrepresenting it persuasively. And it could not misrepresent without representing. This is a much more reasonable complaint against fiction than the complaint that it tells you nothing. The English authoress who in 1810 protested that 'love is a passion particularly exaggerated in novels' could see all that very clearly:

> When a young lady, having imbibed these notions, comes into the world, she finds that this formidable passion acts a very subordinate part on the great theatre of the world; that its vivid sensations are mostly limited to a very early period. . . . Least of all will a course of novels prepare a young lady for the neglect and tedium of life which she is perhaps doomed to encounter. . . .²

The same point was shortly to be substantiated by six novels from the pen of Jane Austen. A century later Ford Madox Ford made it again in more cynical vein, when he remarked of his heroine in *The Good Soldier* (1915) that 'she had read few novels, so that the idea of a pure and constant love succeeding the sound of wedding bells had never been very much presented to her' (IV, i). It is surely as clear as anything could be that novels often mirror a real world, even granting that some mirrors distort. The mother of Brian Moore, the Ulster novelist, on being asked whether she enjoyed reading her son's novels, once replied: 'How *can* I enjoy them? I keep waiting for *me* to come in.'

The simplest and clearest explanation of this mirror function, and an old one, is to call the novelist a kind of historian. That explanation is older than Fielding, who was playfully fond of it. In his essay on Trollope in 1883, James seized on it anew to justify the status of fiction, claiming that the whole dignity of the novel as a convincing fund of knowledge must in the end depend on it. 'It is impossible to imagine what a novelist takes himself to be', he wrote indignantly of Trollope's fictive whimsies such as 'Dear reader', 'unless he regard himself as an historian, and his narrative as history. It is only as an historian that he has the smallest *locus standi*', adding that 'as a narrator of fictitious events' the novelist is simply nowhere. 'To insert into his attempt a backbone of logic, he must relate events that are assumed to be real', and he compares Trollope's nudging apostrophes to the misbehaviour of an actor who disconcertingly pulls off his disguise on stage.

James's argument here is in essence so good that one can learn even from the ways in which it goes wrong. Of course it is true that readers commonly demand of novels that their characters and events should be credible, and of course that kind of credibility is much like what we look for in life itself: whether in the life that goes on around us, or in what the historians tell. Real life, after all, can be bewildering and incredible, in the sense of requiring explanations, and the mere fact that one saw or heard something does not guarantee much in the way of understanding. 'Why on earth did he say that?' one hears people remark, meaning they cannot understand it; or even 'How on earth can he have said it?', meaning that though they heard it they can scarcely believe it. The business of the novelist, to that extent, is like the business of the historian or of any ordinary man. It is to *make sense* of what happens. Macaulay, whom James himself instances here, writes under a demand from his readers that is much like that of a reader of novels, and the parallel grows even closer in fictions that are themselves historical. The Chevalier, or Bonnie Prince Charlie, whether in a history book or in Scott's *Waverley*, needs to be a convincing portrait of an historical personage. It seems not only lunatic to deny this, but profoundly disrespectful to Scott's historical genius and purpose as well.

James's argument is less telling when he attacks Trollope's whimsies or fictive devices. It is interesting to note that James's mistake here is based on a premise similar to that of the post-structuralist critic today, though he would prefer to speak of texts rather than of novels. James believed that the novelist must choose between a descriptive function and a self-regarding or autonomous status, and he disapprovingly quotes a highly fictive remark in the last chapter of Trollope's *Barchester Towers*: 'The end of a novel, like the end of a children's dinner-party, must be made up of sweetmeats and sugar-plums.' That is a plain directive from Trollope to the reader that his novel is a novel, and not a record of real events. But does it represent as complete a difference from history as James or his successors have imagined? Historians frequently signal to their readers that what they are writing is history; and lecturers have been known to begin or end with 'In the present lecture . . .'. In ordinary conversation, in a similar way, it is possible to remark: 'I've something to tell you.' Critics have made such heavy weather of those elements in fiction that announce themselves to be just that, that it is by now difficult to persuade them that such devices, which are at least as old as Rabelais and Cervantes in prose fiction, are in no way peculiar to novels, or even to literature. To use language significantly is to work within contexts; and it can be useful as well as amusing to remind the reader or auditor what that context is. A novelist may find it helpful as well as playful to remind his reader that he is reading a novel: all that can be an essential part of the descriptive force of what is occurring. The fictive is not, or not necessarily, an enemy of the realistic.

As an element in fiction, there is nothing recent about such directive reminders. James, writing in 1883 in his essay on Trollope, abused the device as old-fashioned, which by then it undoubtedly was. But a delight in the fictive would have seemed less surprising to an eighteenth- or nineteenth-century critic than it does to many today. That is perhaps because we are less familiar than they with the rabelaisian and cervantic traditions. Hazlitt, speaking of that riotous compendium on imaginary convents in the Lake District, Thomas Amory's *John Buncle*, which began to appear three years before *Tristram Shandy*, justly remarked that the soul of Rabelais must have passed into its author. Nowadays, if anything like that appeared in English, it would be judged a characteristic product of some *avant-garde* American novelist not yet middle-aged and living west of the Rockies.

★

There is a further weakness in the argument against realism. How far can we confidently assert something to be false without claiming to know what is true? To say that Proust gives us a false picture of the Belle Epoque in Paris, for instance, implies that in some degree we know what an accurate picture would be like. But at this distance in time, we can only know that by report, and one of those reports is Proust's novel. The French New Critics, like other knowledge – sceptics, are inclined to contradict themselves here without noticing it. If fiction never tells the truth about anything – if the claims of literature to describe reality always disappoint, as Roland Barthes once rashly suggested[3] – then we need to be told what better sources of knowledge there are, and on what grounds their claims to superiority rest. Sometimes the sceptic of realism will be able to do just that. But to make his case he will have to be able to do it in every instance, and one counter-instance would be fatal.

★

To restore a community of interest between critic and reader in the present age, then, we need a new Apology for Fiction, and one that respects its power to inform and to instruct. That need not mean any abandonment of interest in narrative form. Form is the *way by which* realities are described: a necessary condition of truth-telling, whether in fiction or elsewhere. Not a sufficient condition, of course. A great liar, like a great artist, needs to be a master of language; and as a contrary we sometimes feel, as in George Orwell's early novels, that the novelist is not a good enough liar – a fumbling sense of form retarding a tale accurate in its general character and worth the telling. But to see form as somehow counterpoised or opposed to the truth of fiction is to miss its point. 'The novel is always subject to a comparison with reality', a critic has remarked of social fiction, 'and therefore found to be illusion'.[4] On the contrary: it is a comparison that honours fiction, which at once needs it and can well sustain it. The difficulty is that some critics have lately demanded too much of description. Indeed, they have put impossible demands upon it. A wider tolerance of its constitution might lead us to demand less.

The first step is to realise that descriptions omit. A map of the London Underground, for instance, describes only the relations between its stations in a linear code, and omits countless details irrelevant to the business of guiding passengers from one station to another. A caricature of a statesman omits more than most oil portraits would do, and still more than his presence would tell us; but if it is a good caricature, or even a merely adequate one, we do not deny that it describes him. The *Mona Lisa*, it seems reasonable to guess, does not reveal everything about the aspect of a Florentine lady living around 1500, and reveals more than that at the same time; but it would be odd to deny that it describes her. Lewis Carroll, in a brilliant summary of the modern argument against realism in *Sylvie and Bruno Concluded* (1893), tells of a map-maker who had 'the grandest idea of all' – a map of a country 'on the scale of *a mile to the mile*', though the farmers objected to spreading it out: 'So now we use the country itself, as its own map, and I assure you it does nearly as well' (ch. 11). A novel that told everything would be about as helpful as Carroll's map. Reality is all the more usefully and efficiently described by selecting the evidence and leaving things out. The second step is to see that a misdescription is a kind of description. Realists have long been under attack for allegedly failing to notice that the novelist himself is a victim of some scheme of values: a theory, a point of view, a conceptual framework, an ideology. It is by now a conventional assumption among the critics of realism that a novelist is always a victim of theory, never its master: an odd assumption, surely, when one considers that many reflective minds such as Flaubert and George Eliot have chosen their convictions in a highly deliberative mood, and that the evidences for their choice survive in what they wrote. Odd, too, in the sense that critics of realism rarely pause to consider that a novelist might understand his world all the better for possessing a conceptual framework or ideology by which to do so. It is still glibly assumed that ideologies can only distort. But it is one thing to accept that they can sometimes do so, and another to assume that they always must. Sometimes, often, we understand the world all the better because of the concepts we bring to that understanding. A map-maker may draw maps all the better for using an inherited framework of latitude and longitude, and it would not be persuasive to object that the lines he draws on his maps are not to be observed on the ground.

The same tolerance should extend to fiction. A novelist may use terms descriptive of social rank in distinguishing his characters, and it would not be much of an objection to protest that such terms would not be understood by those he describes. He might be justified in answering that he claims to be a social novelist precisely because he understands such matters better than others. That claim might prove unfounded, on examination. But it is not in principle absurd. After all, in most areas of human knowledge, such as the physical sciences, we accept without cavil that a professional performance requires a framework of concepts within which to work. The difficulty in accepting something like that in the field of social observation is not impossibly great.

The issue of skill also concerns readers, and the variety of their response is sometimes offered as a reason for doubting the descriptive status of fiction. 'Everybody knows that competent readers read the same text differently', it has been argued, 'which is proof that the text is not fully determined. . . .'[5] But that is a very easy view of what constitutes proof. For one thing, competence is not an absolute attribute, and we might readily accept that, while two readers are competent, one is more so than the other. And for another, a meaning can be determined, in the sense of fixed or stable, without being single or uncomplicated. Many human situations, in life as well as in fiction, have more than one meaning; and it is no objection to the view that they 'have meaning' or meanings to show that one observer or reader emphasises one meaning, and another another.

The assailants of realism are fond of saying that novelists get things wrong. But that objection to realism suggests that the case for its defence has not been understood. What realist in a sober moment ever claimed that he always got everything right? Any descriptive process is subject to error, when human: and all novelists are human. The claim of realism is more moderate than its critics suppose or pretend, and better protected: it holds that the novel, being descriptive, is capable of being right or wrong. It is subject to tests of accuracy. Whether it sustains those tests or not is another matter. Many readers of Flaubert's *Salammbô* or of George Eliot's *Romola* would be ready to argue, and on well-documented grounds, that those novels misdescribe the Carthage of the Punic wars or the Florence of Savonarola. But to argue that is to confirm rather than impair the claims of realism. If such novels did not describe a reality, the question whether they were accurate or inaccurate could not even arise. And it does arise.

★

If the argument for realism holds, then the intelligent reader of novels will need to know about something more than novels. You cannot efficiently judge a description without knowing what it is about. To that extent most novels, and certainly most social novels, are verifiable and falsifiable. That is a conclusion strenuously resisted by formalist critics: indeed formalism might be seen as an escape-hatch from that very claim. They need to be drawn back into the argument, however reluctantly. I believe that formalists are right to sense profound difficulties in the notion that fiction is verifiable, though prone to exaggerate them.

The simplest case of verification is Brian Moore's mother. Since she intimately knows the Ulster world of her son's novels, she might be good at explaining them, and even at explaining what is wrong with them, to anyone who does not. But most acts of novel reading are plainly less assured than that: they more often concern reading a novel that is removed in time, or place, or both. An Englishman reading Jane Austen today would be an instance; an American reading Angus Wilson another. And such cases, which surely represent a majority when taken together, pose difficulties of a higher order. What such instances need is a concept of verification supple enough, and yet firm enough, to accommodate a complex of mental acts with which everyone is in any case familiar. Consider this instance: in his *Lectures on the English Comic Writers* (1819), Hazlitt remarked in Fielding a 'profound knowledge of human nature, at least of English nature; and masterly pictures of the characters of men as he saw them existing', adding that 'as a painter of real life, he was equal to Hogarth'. Since *Joseph Andrews* and *Tom Jones* appeared some thirty years before Hazlitt was born, it is tempting to ask what he knew about it. But he has given part of the answer himself. He knew Hogarth. And he knew Augustan authors other than Fielding, and doubtless some history concerning the reign of George II. His view of the social accuracy of Fielding's novels, then, though vulnerable, is not valueless. In a similar way, an American who is amused by Angus Wilson's *Anglo-Saxon Attitudes* is unlikely to be totally ignorant of twentieth-century England, even if he has never visited it.

A firm yet supple version of the verification theory would not find it hard to explain or justify instances like these. But if it is to work candidly, it must be prepared to avow its own limits. Hazlitt, after all, spoke of human nature rather than of social realism, though his instant qualification 'at least of *English* nature' points towards realism. But humanism, or the doctrine of an unchanging human nature, is a necessary ingredient here. An uninstructed Englishman, after all, can sense a deep affinity between his own nature and Tolstoy's novels, and English fiction can be read with passionate attention by those who have never met an Englishman. One example is a story, told by an anthropologist, of an African child who recently wrote for his village schoolteacher: 'When I first read *Pride and Prejudice*, I asked myself: what have these English ladies to do with me? And then I remembered that, in my own village, there was some one just like Lady Catherine de Burgh.'

★

The case for realism begins by seeing what realism is. It is not a claim to total knowledge or understanding, or even the appearance of those

Salem Academy and College
Gramley Library
Winston-Salem, N.C. 27108

plainly impossible virtues. It does not even need to be that. A witness is said to be the more reliable if he confesses to his own ignorance, and many a realistic novelist has been known to confess his, and to his own advantage. To that extent, at least, the version of realism now under attack is a travesty of some of our greatest fiction. Alain Robbe-Grillet, for instance, in his *Pour un nouveau roman* (1963), has called the novels of Balzac and Stendhal the products of an age when 'everything aimed at imposing the image of a stable, coherent, unequivocal, wholly decipherable universe' (p. 31). But the reader will search Balzac and Stendhal in vain for any claim, explicit or otherwise, that they saw their social world as totally decipherable – '*déchiffrable*'. What the realist does claim, needs to claim and can reasonably claim, is to know something; and it is odd that the difference between knowing something and knowing everything needs to be explained, especially since all of us are instances of it. 'To be realistic', Trollope once sensibly remarked, 'you must know accurately that which you describe.'[6] That is nothing like a claim to omniscience. When Flaubert, in a famous letter about *Madame Bovary*, compared the artist to 'God in creation – invisible yet all-powerful' (19 February 1857), he was summarising how a novelist might ideally appear to a reader, not claiming a godlike knowledge of anything, even of his own provincial Normandy: 'We must sense him everywhere, but never see him.' The claim to know what you know is nothing like a claim to know everything.

Robbe-Grillet's argumentative trick here is ultimately a vulgar one, though dignified by logicians under the lofty title of the Higher Re-definition. It consists of putting unrealistic conditions on realism, 'upping the price' on what constitutes description; and then demonstrating that these extravagant conditions have not been met and even, in the nature of things, cannot be met. But the claims of realism are more moderate than this. 'The task of the modern novel', Theodor Fontane once remarked, 'seems to me to be a description of a life, a society, a group of people, as the undistorted reflection of the life we lead.' And the word 'task' is highly significant here: it is an aspiration only sometimes to be achieved.

★

The claim to understand the world around us is now commonly identified with the ideology of liberalism. It may be granted at once that some of the greatest realists have been liberals: Constant, Stendhal, Dickens, Manzoni, Trollope, George Eliot, Meredith and E. M. Forster. But it is surely too high a compliment to the liberal mind to imply that it, and it alone among the great ideologies, is capable of observing and describing reality efficiently, or of trying to do so. Those who argue that, paradoxically enough, are not usually liberals themselves, and they need to be invited to see how much they are conceding to an opposing view. They should also be asked to notice how many great conservative novelists have written in the tradition of the real: Fielding, Jane Austen, Goethe, Scott, Balzac. . . . The liberal preponderance is an arguable claim in the nineteenth century and since. But liberals did not create realism: it existed before the 1830s. They exploited it magisterially – an inheritance from others.

It is equally implausible to suggest that only liberals believe social description to be possible and accurate today. Conservatives and Marxists, on occasion, plainly believe in that possibility too. When the Peking government abuses Soviet society, it evidently believes it has understood its nature and is capable of describing and explaining it. The Vatican does not often suppose that it lacks the capacity to understand or convey the nature and causes of what it holds to be modern social degeneracy. We all believe we can describe, when it matters. Those who argue that social knowledge, and the moral judgements that often accompany it, are merely personal and of no objective standing seldom talk as if that principle applied to themselves, or to factions or governments they hate or admire. The critical argument against the truth-status of fiction as knowledge would impress more if it grew less parochial in its assumptions, more observant of the world that novels describe, and readier to follow argument candidly where it leads.

There is evidently something titillating about a claim to ignorance. It cocks a snook, for one thing, at those who claim to know. Since '*to write* is an intransitive verb', Roland Barthes has provocatively declared, 'literature is always unrealistic'.[7] A remark to read with a smile, and likely to have been written with one. But we cannot evade the real so easily, or smile our way forever out of seeing what fiction can do to explain it. The real exists independently of what critics of literature may say: it stands forever untouched by disclaimers. 'The world, unfortunately, is real; and I, unfortunately, am Borges.'[8] It will take more than a school of letters to unpeople the universe.

NOTES

1. Sidney Lanier, *The English Novel* (New York: 1891) p. 4.

2. Anna Barbauld, 'On the Origin and Progress of Novel-Writing', prefixed to *British Novelists* (London: 1810) pp. 50–1.

3. Roland Barthes, preface to Bruce Morrissette, *Les Romans de Robbe-Grillet* (Paris: 1963) p. 14.

4. Edward W. Said, 'Molestation and Authority in Narrative Fiction', in J. Hillis Miller (ed.) *Aspects of Narrative* (New York: 1971) p. 49.

5. Frank Kermode, *How We Read Novels* (Southampton: 1975) p. 15.

6. Anthony Trollope, *Thackeray* (1879) p. 185.

7. 'Écrivains et écrivants', in *Essais critiques* (Paris: 1964) p. 149.

8. Jorge Luis Borges, 'A New Refutation of Time' (1946), translated in his *Labyrinths* (Harmondsworth: 1970) p. 269.

2 *Memoirs*

The three grand forms of European fiction, in broadly historical order, have been the memoir-novel, the letter-novel, and the novel in the third person. They might be represented diagrammatically by the three personal pronouns *I*, *you* and *he*: the memoir being characterised by *I*, the letter by *you*, and the novel of the third person by *he* and *she*. In this chapter I shall consider the first of them.

★

The memoir or I-novel, fashionable in the early eighteenth century in France and England, is composed in the form of an autobiography, and in the first person; the novelist himself, if he appears at all, claiming to be no more than the editor of papers that happen to have come into his possession. Like the letter-novel, the memoir is often based on some variant of the convention of the 'old oak chest': the 'editor' claiming, most commonly in a preface, to have found some forgotten manuscripts in a cupboard, attic or box, or to have stumbled on them in a roadway, and to have edited or translated them.

The *Adolphe* (1816) of Benjamin Constant, written in 1806–7, provides a late but classic instance. It opens with a pretended 'Note by the Publisher' (*Avis de l'éditeur*) that explains how, years before, he had met a melancholy stranger in a Calabrian village, later receiving from the innkeeper a box containing his letters, as well as the portrait of a woman and a notebook 'containing the anecdote or story you are about to read', all without any forwarding address. Years after he showed the story to friends in Germany, and was persuaded by one of them to publish it 'without changing a word of the original' – the novel ending with a 'Letter to the Publisher' (*Lettre à l'éditeur*) from the friend in Germany, vouching for the truth of the story and urging him to publish it as a warning example against the love of older women.

There is also a Reply (*Réponse*) by the publisher reinforcing the moral point that strength of character counts for more than intelligence. Since the novel is in some sense autobiographical, being based on Constant's own unhappy love affair with Mme de Staël, among others, the tactic here may amount to an ingenious double bluff. By the early nineteenth century the devices of the memoir-novel were shopworn to the point that it was only needful to call a novel a genuine memoir to provoke sophisticated disbelief. And in this case there was some point in bluffing: when the novel appeared Mme de Staël, who was only eighteen months older than Constant, still had a year to live.

In its continuous life, the memoir-novel arose in seventeenth-century France: an apt time and place, since the French memoir was an established literary form in the reign of Louis XIV. The fictional memoir throve, of necessity, on a taste for the real thing, and arose out of that taste. Its first English master was Defoe, its first masterpiece his *Robinson Crusoe* (1719). The classic opening of such novels is that of autobiography itself: 'I was born . . .', and *Crusoe* begins in classic style:

> I was born in the year 1632, in the city of York, of a good family, though not of that country, my father being a foreigner from Bremen who settled first at Hull. He got a good estate by merchandise, and leaving off his trade lived afterward at York, from whence he had married my mother, whose relations were named Robinson

adding the irresistible detail that his father's name, and at first his own, had been Kreutznaer. Defoe had already edited genuine memoirs, and did not attempt fiction until he was nearly sixty; and given that the English were already reading more or less authentic stories by travellers who had lived in remote and desolate places, it is unsurprising if *Crusoe* were supposed by many of its first readers to be a genuine account, and attacked by others as spurious. Defoe replied ambiguously to these attacks in *Serious Reflections during the Life of Robinson Crusoe* (1720), maintaining that his novel was historical as well as 'allegorical', and teasingly remarking in his preface that the book relates to 'a man alive, and well known too' – in which case, presumably, his name was not Robinson Crusoe. *Crusoe* sets the pace in memoir-fiction: it even combines its two principal forms, autobiography and diary, a fictional memoir being interspersed with 'Extracts from the Journal', supposedly written at the time.

The memoir-novel often claims to be a true memoir or journal on its very title-page. Grimmelshausen's *Simplicissimus* (1669), a German novel set in the Thirty Years' War, proclaims itself in its title as by 'German Schleifheim', and ends with a report by a Dutch sea-captain on how he obtained the manuscript. But Schleifheim's claim is denied in the postscript or 'Beschluss', which is initialled 'HICVG' – an anagram, like Schleifheim itself and Simplex's 'real' name, of Grimmelshausen's own. These elaborate devices concealed the true authorship of the novel for well over a century. Half a century after *Simplicissimus*, *Crusoe* was to be entitled as 'written by himself'; and Defoe's next novel, *Memoirs of a Cavalier* (1720) was subtitled *a military journal of the wars in Germany, and the wars in England, from the year 1632 to the year 1648*; while *Moll Flanders*, where Defoe adopts the voice of a woman, is subtitled *written from her own memorandums*, though Defoe's claim in his preface is designedly ambiguous:

> The world is so taken up of late with novels and romances, that it will be hard for a private history to be taken for genuine, where the names and other circumstances of the person are concealed; and on this account we must be content to leave the reader to pass his own opinion upon the ensuing sheets, or take it much as he pleases,

admitting, however, to having edited the imaginary manuscript heavily: '. . . the original of this story is put into new words, and the style . . . is a little altered' to save the blushes of polite readers – Moll having learned bad language in gaol.

Avowals like these can hardly have been intended to deceive. But other memoir-novels could be accepted as genuine by intelligent opinion and for a long time – and may even have been so, or nearly so: in which case, one would be inclined to add, their status as novels needs to be questioned. Defoe's *Capt. Carleton* (1728) was accepted by Johnson and by Scott, who edited it in 1808, as the genuine memoir of an English officer serving from 1672 to the Peace of Utrecht in 1713; and modern scholarship has in part returned to something like this conclusion. But if Defoe edited a real memoir, the instance might still be accepted as borderline as between fact and fiction, depending on the extent of his editing. Scott was not incapable of being deceived in such matters, though he was fond of parodying the memoir-novel himself; his introduction to *The Fortunes of Nigel* (1822), for example, is written as by a Captain Clutterbuck to a Dr Dryasdust, and includes an imaginary dialogue with himself as the 'Author of *Waverley*'. And the modern reader might be forgiven for feeling uncertain about the exact status of Diderot's *La Religieuse*, a scandalous account of events in a convent, some of it true, which Diderot wrote in 1760, though it was not published until after his death.

On the whole, and to an increasing degree in the eighteenth century, novelists wish their claim to genuineness in a memoir-novel not to be accepted. There were several reasons for this. One was that the status of prose fiction was itself rising: claims to classic standing and artistic significance were being made, and perhaps accepted, at least as early as Fielding's in the 1740s. Another was that the playful possibilities of transparent deceit were growing more widely and variously understood. Sterne's *Life and Opinions of Tristram Shandy* (1760–7) is a vast and elaborate parody of the fictional memoir in which, by the end, the hero has not been born. The very title of Goldsmith's only novel is a transparent fiction: *The Vicar of Wakefield: a Tale Supposed To Be Written by Himself* (1766), with a prefatory Advertisement signed Oliver Goldsmith, apologising in his own name of 'an hundred faults in this thing'. Henry Mackenzie's *Man of Feeling* (1771), which appeared when the vogue was fading, claims in an introduction to be all that was left after a sporting curate had used some of the manuscript as gun-wadding, so that the novel amounts to some disordered chapters starting with 'Chapter XI' – an ingenious way for a young Scotsman in London to sell off a bundle of sketches to a publisher.

By the nineteenth century, the convention is moribund, though it still has its occasional triumphs like *Adolphe*, and it can still be a matter for playful allusion. Dickens, writing his first novel, *The Posthumous Papers of the Pickwick Club* (1836–7), at first within a scheme not wholly of his own choosing, begins with a whimsical reference to himself as an editor of the minutes of an imaginary club for London gentlemen:

> The first ray of light which illumines the gloom . . . is derived from the perusal of the following entry in the Transactions of the Pickwick Club, which the editor of these papers feels the highest pleasure in laying before his readers, as a proof of the careful attention . . . with which his search among the multifarious documents confided to him has been conducted.
>
> May 12, 1827. Joseph Smiggers . . . presiding . . . ,

followed by the resolutions agreed to. In this instance the minutes of a society were evidently felt to offer publisher and illustrator wider opportunities than the memoir of one man. In the event, they gave rise to the greatest comic novel in the language, though one that alludes to the old convention of a discovered cache of manuscripts only once again – in the third chapter. A modest allusion: to read *Pickwick* is to watch a tradition all but dead grasped and transformed as if by a giant's hand.

Dickens was an avid reader of eighteenth-century fiction, at least in youth; and in the most clearly autobiographical of his novels, *David Copperfield* (1850), he was to revive the memoir in a manner at once facetious and deadly serious. On the wrapper of the monthly parts, in 1849–50, the novel is entitled *The Personal History, Adventures, Experiences and Observations of David Copperfield the Younger, of Blunderstone Rookery (which he never meant to be published on any account)*, though on the title-page itself, and for the volume issue of 1850, the novel was more conveniently called *The Personal History of David Copperfield*. The words in parenthesis are a clear if jocular allusion to the old oak chest, though the novel lacks the customary preface or postscript to support that convention. That might have seemed unnecessarily obvious, by 1850. But its first chapter is called 'I Am Born', and its first sentence gives an odd, and utterly romantic, twist to the tradition, while the second restores it momentarily to its original function of a pretended autobiography:

> Whether I shall turn out to be the hero of my own life, or whether that station will be held by anybody else, these pages must show. To begin my life with the beginning of my life, I record that I was born (as I have been informed and believe) on a Friday, at twelve o'clock at night,

and the most original stroke of the book recalls in maturity the distinct and unique nature of a child's consciousness – a feat unattempted in eighteenth-century fiction, and vividly predictive of Proust and Joyce. 'The first objects that assume a distinct presence before me', the second chapter begins (it is entitled 'I Observe'), 'as I look far back into the blank of my infancy, are my mother . . . and Peggotty . . .', and the very dimensions of the house are recalled with the eye of a child: 'Here is a long passage – what a perspective I make of it! – leading from Peggotty's kitchen. . .'. Even a child's reading is of its own kind, and convincingly childish. In the fourth chapter, oppressed by a stepfather, David is sent upstairs, to read Cervantes, Lesage, Defoe and Smollett: 'I have been Tom Jones (a child's Tom Jones, a harmless creature) for a week together. . .'. This is to see a possibility that the pioneers of the memoir-novel could not themselves see: of an awareness not yet adult, and suggestive of a character still to be formed. For a century or more the I-novel had borne within itself a prospect of analysis that a Victorian genius was the first fully to perceive and exploit.

Long before 1800 the memoir-novel had ceased to be fashionable, though not to be numerous, and its decay was long and glorious. The oak-chest formula can survive even in third-person narrative after 1800, often as an ironically distancing device. Manzoni's *I promessi sposi* (1827), for example, begins with an introduction in archaic and highly rhetorical Italian, as if copied from a seventeenth-century manuscript, which Manzoni pretends to break off, exclaiming that no one nowadays will have the patience to read such stuff; and he promptly switches into modern Italian, referring occasionally in the course of the novel to an anonymous chronicler with an odd taste for laboured similes, or dropping the phrase 'as the manuscript says' ('*come dice il manoscritto*'). In the last paragraph of the book he calls himself the repairer ('*racconciatore*') of his imaginary source. A tradition is fading into mere decoration. Thackeray's *Pendennis* (1849–50) and *The Virginians* (1858–9) have 'editors', though they are mentioned only rarely: 'All this narrative', Thackeray assures us perfunctorily in *Pendennis*, 'is taken from Pen's own confessions' (ch. 20); and George Warrington, at the end of *The Virginians*, has his confessions about married life suddenly cut short, in a bid for moral privacy that masks the novelist's own striving after decency: 'Here three pages are torn out of Sir George Warrington's MS book, for which the editor is sincerely sorry' (ch. 85). *The Newcomes* (1854), in a similar way, is supposedly based on the yellowing pages of Clive Newcome's log. But Thackeray's most sustained imitation of the memoir is *Henry Esmond* (1852), entitled *The History of Henry Esmond Esq. Written by Himself,* and the Queen Anne style of the book was even mimicked typographically in the first edition with a long 's', though the dedication is signed by Thackeray: a more highly sustained exercise in pastiche than Rose Macaulay's Civil War novel, *They Were Defeated* (1932), if only because Addison's English is easier to imitate than Jeremy Taylor's or Sir Thomas Browne's.

But instances such as these, from the past hundred years, are only sparsely numbered. Between 1854 and 1879–80 Gottfried Keller, the greatest of Swiss novelists in German, turned *Der grüne Heinrich* from a third-person novel containing a long first-person narration into one radically in the first person: a strange technical reversion that suggests the romantic potentialities of fictional autobiography. And in 1906 William de Morgan, already in his sixties, produced his first novel, *Joseph Vance,* protectively subtitled *an ill-written autobiography* and ending with a 'Note by the Editor' that tells how the manuscript came into his hands, along with a 'Postscript by the Publishers' and a letter supposed to have been misdirected in the post, establishing the identity of a character in the novel. But then de Morgan, whose late success astonished even himself, described himself as a Dickens man 'blundered into the wrong generation', and more recent exercises have been marked by a high literary sophistication designed to salvage a discarded tradition. Proust's vast novel, composed in the first person, revives the memoir as a modern confessional. Robert Graves's *I, Claudius* (1934) is offered as a translation of an imaginary autobiography of a Roman emperor: a work technically straightforward, and based on some genuine classical scholarship. Hermann Broch's *Death of Virgil* (1945), composed in German by a Viennese refugee, imagines the Roman poet on his deathbed, ruminating the state of civilisation and the question whether he should order his *Aeneid* to be burnt. And Thomas Mann's *Dr Faustus* (1947) is subtitled 'told by a friend' ('*erzählt von einem Freunde*') who bears the improbable name of Serenus Zeitblom; he tells the life of the composer Adrian Leverkühn, who wrote music under the Devil's influence and died in imbecility: a cool account of the growth of the twentieth-century German mind through Nietzsche and Wagner into a state of devilish possession in the 1930s.

The memoir lives, then, if fitfully, in fiction. It has flourished even since the turn of the half century. R. C. Hutchinson's *Recollection of a Journey* (1952) is the nightmare tale of a Polish woman suffering the horrors of Nazi and Communist tyranny in the Second World War. Three of the four novels comprising Lawrence Durrell's *Alexandrian Quartet* (1957–60) are in the first person, the narrator using the diaries of other characters, at times, but remaining nameless throughout the first novel, *Justine.* And John Barth's *Giles Goat-boy* (1966) claims to be based on a taped autobiography of an academic, beginning with a 'Publisher's Disclaimer', four editors' reports and a cover-letter debating the authorship of the text; and it ends with a postscript contesting the authenticity of the text and a footnote drawing attention to a disparity between the printing types used in the postscript and the cover-letter. Ezra Pound once remarked of *Tristram Shandy* that nobody had better try to write it again. But novelists do sometimes try to write it again. One of the best things to do with the memoir as a radical device in modern fiction is to make learned fun of it.

★

The memoir-novel merges almost insensibly into novels recounted, in whole or part, by a pretended source of knowledge such as an observer or an historian. At the earliest, such figures can stand outside the story altogether as part of the third-person narrative. *Don Quixote* (1605–15), for example, includes a narrator who is named as the author of the prefaces: an Arab historian called Cid Hamet Benengeli to whose imaginary manuscript Cervantes pretends to refer, from time to time, to finish parts of his story – an infidel author intruding into a third-person novel. Congreve's *Incognita* (1700) has a narrator, though too shadowy a figure to be clearly differentiated from the author. And with Marivaux and Fielding the narrator can become a sort of ironised figure of the novelist himself, and with Sterne a crackbrained version of the author: aspects of a debt to Cervantes more profound than the formula of a master–servant pair wandering across a landscape.

Some narrators are plainly unreliable, at least in the sense that their judgements are not wholly recommended by the novelist. Diderot's nun in *La Religieuse*, who tells the story, is a nineteen-year-old Catholic girl, though Diderot was a middle-aged freethinker when he wrote it. Old Thady, the family retainer who relates Maria Edgeworth's *Castle Rackrent* (1800), is a world away from Miss Edgeworth in age, religion and dialect, though she offers him as an engaging representative of a vanished age. Other narrators, like Constant's Adolphe, may be offered with an air of irony that masks a perilously literal purpose. Ford Madox Ford's masterpiece, *The Good Soldier* (1915), is recounted as if by a prosy old American whose wife has betrayed him with the hero of the novel. Sartre's *La Nausée* (1938) begins with a brief introduction signed by editors whose identity we never discover, in a device that may be presumed a disclaimer on the part of the novelist. And the form lives on, as in J. D. Salinger's *Catcher in the Rye* (1951), which is composed as if by a teenage American; and in several of Iris Murdoch's novels, notably the first, *Under the Net* (1954).

The device cannot always be seen as a disclaimer. Some narrators are simply all there is of a novel, so that it would be as odd to doubt their word as to doubt Crusoe's. The character known as the Old Man or 'Vieillard' in Bernardin de Saint-Pierre's *Paul et Virginie* (1787) tells all there is of the story, including some things he could hardly have known, such as Virginie's inmost thoughts; and Anne Brontë's *Tenant of Wildfell Hall* (1848) is largely a long diary from a single hand, enclosed in a letter from another. None of that forbids an element of irony, for those determined to see it; but that determination can be misplaced, and irony does not function best without a frame. Nelly Dean, the old retainer in Emily Brontë's *Wuthering Heights* (1847), tells of events she has seen, heard or heard of and, so far as mind can, seemingly understood, and she even reports what she cannot claim to understand at all; Lockwood, the visitor to rural Yorkshire to whom she tells her story, appears to accept it, and it is hard to see what else the reader can do but accept it too, or cast the book away. The observer–narrator, though he distances the action from the novelist, is by no means always an ironic device. He may license mystery, or fantasy; but his account can remain credible, even gripping, in its own terms. And even the credence a reader gives to fantasy is still credence of a kind: Gobineau's *Les Pléiades* (1874), for example, begins with a travel diary set in Switzerland, before it turns into three narrators telling their stories in intertwining plots, in a pattern reminiscent of the *Arabian Nights*. For all the thick patina of dialect used by Mark Twain in *Huckleberry Finn* (1885), it would be self-defeating not to accept the boy's own version of what happened. The novel, which followed *Tom Sawyer* by nine years, begins:

> You don't know about me without you have read a book by the name of *The Adventures of Tom Sawyer*, but that ain't no matter. That book was made by Mr Mark Twain and he told the truth, mainly. . . .

But that irony is double-edged: since there is no truth about Tom Sawyer outside what Mark Twain wrote, such novels might be said to tell the truth altogether. So does the narrator who tells the story of his friend in Alain Fournier's *Le Grand Meaulnes* (1915); so do Raymond Chandler's Marlowe stories, told as by a private detective whose wry, sentimental puritanism the author surely endorses; and so does Samuel Beckett's Molloy trilogy (1951-3), where the mind of the narrator is the total action of the novels, though not Beckett's mind.

The designedly difficult territories lie elsewhere, and they are not confined to novels in the first person. How far does Maria Edgeworth endorse the judgements of Old Thady in *Castle Rackrent*, or Henry James that of his 'central intelligences' in his later, third-person fiction? Or how far does Conrad endorse Marlow's view in *The Heart of Darkness* (1902)? How much is the reader asked to swallow; and how much is he invited to believe there are truths beyond those that are suggested or told? The likeliest answer here, in cases of the unreliable (or possibly unreliable) narrator, is that the whole truth exceeds his account without invalidating it. In *The Heart of Darkness* all we know of Kurtz's death in the Congo is from Marlow's report, which is itself based on reports; Marlow is moved and puzzled by the symbolism of what he knows, but his puzzlement may be partly Conrad's too. By the decades around 1900, in James, Conrad and Proust, a new possibility arises out of the struggle between truth and clarity in stories: the possibility that the novelist may grope for significance along with the reader, certain of his tale but uncertain of its significance, or all of it, and ready to share with others a bewildering richness of sense.

The novel in the first person, as it emerges out of the pseudo-memoir, can work through a single voice like Crusoe's or Adolphe's, or through more than one, in polyphony. *Wuthering Heights* has two narrators, but Nelly Dean so far outweighs Lockwood as to turn him into a receiving instrument to her tale. But Wilkie Collins's *Moonstone* (1868), which is essentially the first of detective novels, consists of a number of first-person accounts of a single crime, so that it is like listening to the answers of one witness after another; and William Faulkner's early novel of 1929, *The Sound and the Fury*, has the first of its four parts 'told by an idiot', Benjy, who has no sense of time, and the next two by each of his brothers – while the fourth part, which explains everything, is omnisciently narrated. No wonder if the lazy have been known to read it first.

If all this can be seen as a long ancestral descent, then the tradition of fictional memoir cannot be called dead. But there is still a powerful, if subtle difference between a novel that asks to be confused with real events, like *Crusoe* or *Moll*, and one that offers itself as pure fiction, like *The Good Soldier* or *Le Grand Meaulnes*. That difference is not significantly weakened, though it is teasingly confused, by the fact that

Ford's novel and Alain-Fournier's are both highly autobiographical in content. Where Defoe offered an invention as a truth, they offer a truth, or partial truth, as invention. The contrast remains ineffaceable and very great.

If that distinction is accepted, then the vogue of the memoir–novel can be seen as a limited one, and there can be no doubt when it flourished best. It arose in the wake of the real memoir or autobiography in the late seventeenth century, and played a major role in prose fiction in the first half of the eighteenth. Out of nearly 1000 works of French fiction in that half century, it has been estimated, nearly 200 are in the first person singular, though not all are memoirs, with about fifty collections of letters, including letter-novels, in the same period.[1] Similar figures for English fiction are not available; but the epistolary form, like the memoir, entered French before English, and it seems natural to assume that the memoir dominated the Augustan novel, too. The *conte* or tale, which is a briefer work, is another matter: it was born of a match between the fairy tale and the oriental tale, and was almost always, as in Voltaire's *Candide* (1759) or Johnson's *Rasselas* (1759), in the third person. But in French usage a *conte* is not a *roman*, and it might be useful to translate that convention into English, which is less precise here in its terms, and to insist that a tale is not a novel. In that case, all but a few major novels before 1800 are either memoirs or letters, unless they are buttressed by some special critical justification, as in Fielding. *Joseph Andrews* (1742) and *Tom Jones* (1749) are both in the third person; indeed, Fielding had mercilessly parodied Richardson's fondness for letters in *Shamela* (1741), if his authorship of that parody can now be considered certain, and he was never to attempt a memoir-novel. But then both *Andrews* and *Jones* are justified by prefaces that claim for themselves the sanction of Aristotle's *Poetics*: they are comic epics in prose, so Fielding argues, or modern versions of Homer's lost epic; and the epic is after all a third-person form. Smollett's *Lancelot Greaves* (1762) is cervantic, or based on the imposing European model of *Don Quixote* (1605–15), which in its turn is a parody of medieval romance; and romance is a third-person form. But Smollett's first novel, *The Adventures of Roderick Random* (1748), had been composed in the predominating style of a memoir, and begins in the classic manner of *Crusoe* a generation earlier: 'I was born in the northern part of this united kingdom . . .', so that the reader knows in an instant that he is reading the pretended autobiography of a Scotsman who was born after the Union of 1707. (Smollett himself, who adapts his own recollections in the novel, especially of his naval experiences, was born in Dumbartonshire in 1721.)

★

Random is highly episodic. So, after all, are most genuine autobiographies; and so are most lives. The point deserves some emphasis since the episodic form is as natural to the memoir-novel as to the cervantic or the picaresque, and the three are by now susceptible to various confusions. The cervantic novel, ultimately deriving from *Don Quixote*, is a satirical form hostile to romance and to heroic pretension, emphasising the claims of the real against the unreal, and it most commonly concerns an innocent master and his more worldly servant, such as Quixote and Sancho Panza, encountering absurd adventures on their travels. That model is subject to variations: in Fielding's *Joseph Andrews*, for example, it is the master who is fat and the servant lean, though in *Quixote* it had been the reverse; and Fielding's inversion is adopted by Dickens nearly a century later in *Pickwick*, where a fat Mr Pickwick employs a lean Mr Weller.

The picaresque novel is a distinct form, and begins, in the same land and age as *Quixote*, with Alemán's *Guzmán de Alfarache* (1599–1604), where an erring servant to many masters sins and ultimately repents, the last page releasing him from the life of a galley slave. (Some would date the convention still earlier, to the anonymous *Lazarillo de Tormes* of 1554.) The tradition is softened in Lesage, Defoe and Smollett – at once humanised and sentimentalised – and such characters as Moll Flanders, Gil Blas and, still more, Roderick Random and Tom Jones, are arguably more sinned against than sinning; and they end their lives, after wild adventures, in a happiness that is not felt to be undeserved. If the term 'picaresque' is widened to include them, as by convention it is, then some picaresque novels are indeed memoir-novels, though by no means all memoir-novels are picaresque. Though picaresque novels are often episodic, so are many others: the fact is in no clear sense a distinguishing characteristic. And neither one nor the other should be confused with the cervantic novel, where the hero, like Fielding's Parson Adams, is a victim of innocent illusions about the virtue of mankind.

★

The constraints of the memoir are clear, and they help to explain its decline in the eighteenth century. For one, the first person does not permit a novelist to carry his narrative to its natural conclusion in the death of its hero or heroine – a task for which he needs to resort to a preface or postscript. 'We cannot say, indeed', Defoe knowingly remarks in his preface to *Moll Flanders,*

> that this history is carried on quite to the end of the life of this famous Moll Flanders, as she calls herself, for nobody can write their own life to the full end of it, unless they can write it after they are dead . . .

so that the novel ends with Moll's return to England from Virginia happily and virtuously married, with an editorial note 'Written in the year 1683'. Herman Melville's *Moby Dick* (1851), perhaps the last great memoir-novel in English to subject itself openly to this constraint, ends with the sinking of the *Pequod* and an epilogue explaining how the narrator Ishmael escaped the suction of the sinking ship by the happy appearance of a floating coffin, in which he lay for a day and a night unscathed by shark or sea hawk, until picked up by a passing ship. This will pass in the high symbolic world that Melville has created here, in a fervour little short of allegorical. But it also suggests, in its straining ingenuity, the death of a form. By and large autobiography is more constricting than biography, and by 1800 the temptation to adopt the third person must have looked overwhelming.

Again, there is a taxing confusion in the memoir that concerns suspense. If the hero claims to recall events that have already occurred, then he knows the outcome of those events in a manner quite unlike the experience of living through them. Defoe's Moll, as she is imagined writing her own life, must already know that at one point in her past career she unwittingly married her own brother. To be sure, it is only on one interpretation of story-telling that the suspense is the greater if the reader is ignorant of the result, and Moll's misalliance is proclaimed in the very title-page. But granted that the novelist accepts that interpretation of suspense, it is difficult to see how he can reconcile such ignorance with the writing of a memoir unless by supposing the author to be engaged in a conscious deceit of the reader. That may be a pleasing deceit, for a time; but it is a pleasure liable to fade with familiarity. In the third person, by contrast, it is a matter of choice for the novelist whether he should reveal the end in the beginning or conceal it. The modern novelist commands his own fictions in a way many of his forbears did not.

And finally, an autobiographer, real or imagined, can only recount what he has himself seen and heard or, by a natural extension, sensed or guessed or been told of what he or others have seen or heard. Unlike the invisible narrtor who writes in the third person, he is not an eye or ear in every wall of every room, or a spy even in the minds and hearts of his own characters. This is a limitation that applies even more strongly to the memoir-novels than to the epistolary, where letters may be written by a wide variety of characters, and where a many-sided narrative is easier to wield and to grasp. The problem in the memoir is admittedly susceptible to partial solutions of many kinds, including dialogue; but then it is only because the novel pretends to be a memoir that it is a problem at all. A difficulty needs to earn its keep: does this? In James Hogg's *Private Memoirs and Confessions of a Justified Sinner* (1824), the difficulty is solved by doubling the narration; the title continues *written by himself, with a detail of curious traditionary facts and other evidence by the editor.* 'Traditionary' means by hearsay, or at second hand; and the novel is divided, for much the greater part, into two. The first and somewhat shorter section is entitled 'The Editor's Narrative', in the third person, and ends with the strange disappearance of the hero – villain Wringhim, who has sold his soul to the Devil. Hogg then writes, as in the person of an editor:

> I have now the pleasure of presenting my readers with an original document of a most singular nature, and preserved for their perusal in a still more singular manner. I offer no remarks on it, and make as few additions to it, leaving every one to judge for himself. We have heard much of the rage of fanaticism in former days, but nothing to this. . . .

and follows with the 'Private Memoirs and Confessions' themselves, as written by Wringhim in the first person, 'My life has been a life of trouble and turmoil . . .', which occupies most of the novel; ending with a letter that had already appeared in *Blackwood's Magazine*, signed 'James Hogg', and some concluding remarks by the imaginary writer, who carefully distinguishes himself from Hogg, telling how the manuscript of the confession was procured and published.

It cannot be denied that, whether because of these elaborations or in spite of them, the story of a devil-possessed Scottish Calvinist clearly emerges. On the other hand, there are moments when Hogg's ingenuity verges here on the incredible. The reader can accept that Wringhim might write of the moment when he is exposed as a liar, 'My cheek burnt with offence, rather than shame', since it is possible for a man to know he is blushing, and above all to know why. But at the end of the 'Confessions', which are wound up as a diary for 1712, the tale is implausibly brought to a close at a moment preceding death itself:

> My hour is at hand. – Almighty God, what is this that I am about to do! The hour of repentance is past . . . I will now seal up my little book . . .

Similarly, in Diderot's *La Religieuse*, which is recounted by a young nun, a lesbian experience with a Mother Superior is described as by one who is still innocent; and in a more recent instance, Ford's *The Good Soldier* (1915), a foolish elderly observer offers long and implausibly intimate accounts of the motives of others, and recounts events he can only have known at second hand, and which only a highly intelligent man could have understood in that fashion. Occasionally Ford recollects the difficulty: 'God knows what Leonora said . . .', he makes his narrator remark (IV, iv), as if recalling himself to the constraints of his own technique. The limitation is galling.

For all that, memoir is a pattern of fiction that remains a possibility to this day. F. Scott Fitzgerald composed his first novel, *This Side of Paradise* (1920), in the first person, but later changed to the third on the advice of his publisher. The option is still open, and still occasionally taken. Iris Murdoch's *The Sea, the Sea* (1978) begins with a paragraph of memoir and then slips into what it calls a diary; and her first novel, *Under the Net* (1954), was dominated by the first person. But such instances look striking, and almost nostalgic, in the present age. Long before Hogg wrote his only novel, or Dickens his first, the high fashion of the memoir had been played out.

NOTE

1. S. P. Jones, *A List of French Prose Fiction 1700–1750* (New York: 1939), introduction.

3 *Letters*

The second species of novel based on the 'old oak chest' of discovered manuscripts is the letter-novel or epistolary novel, where the author poses as an editor of letters that have somehow come into his possession.

The origin of the form is obscure and even difficult to define, since collections of real or imaginary letters could be used in Renaissance Europe as elegant handbooks of instruction. These sometimes include anecdotes and even, as part of those anecdotes, dialogue; and fictional stories as well as true can be told in them. The earliest letter-novels may be fifteenth-century Spanish, and from unknown hands, but their earliest history cannot be convincingly mapped.

The natural starting-point for all Europe is the *Lettres d'une religieuse portugaise* (1669), now believed to be the original fiction of Lavergne de Guilleragues, though long supposed to be what they claim to be: a translation into French of five lost letters from a Portuguese nun to a French officer, a lover who had abandoned her. But even if there was such a nun, and even if Guilleragues had access to some originals now lost, it seems clear that the book is substantially a novel; and when it first appeared in English in 1678, as *Portuguese Letters*, it represented the first notable instance in the language of a novel told exclusively in an epistolary form.

The first such novel to be composed originally in English, it seems likely, was Aphra Behn's *Love-letters between a Nobleman and His Sister*, which began to appear five years later, in 1683. Again, the status of the instance is not utterly clear. It may have been based on a real, or at least rumoured, case of aristocratic incest. But as with the *Portuguese Letters*, it is a reasonable guess that the work is radically a fiction, even if based on true events.

Both Guilleragues and Aphra Behn gave Europe what are fundamentally studies in high sentiment – and above all models of how language can best be used to convey sentiment. Their books are love manuals. To that extent, as least, they do not utterly lose contact with the Renaissance handbook; and both being concerned with illicit love, they help to explain Samuel Richardson's insistence, some sixty years later, that the novel urgently needed to be rescued from the imputation of a profound moral taint. Like the memoir-novel, then, the epistolary arises out of something truthful and instructive; and like it, it clings to a memory of its own origins and for long claims to be real.

Letter-novels were abundant in English as well as French before Richardson produced the first English classic, *Pamela*, in 1740. An historian has estimated that, of about 1000 works of prose fiction in English between the Restoration of 1660 and *Pamela* eighty years later, over 200 were letter-fiction: a proportion of one-fifth and more which, surprisingly enough, is not less than it was to prove in the heyday of the epistolary from 1740 to 1800.[1] Its first English master is Richardson, who confines himself to it in his three great novels of 1740–54; it is mercilessly mocked by Fielding in *Shamela* in 1741, an attack on Richardson's *Pamela*; it is the form of Rousseau's *Julie: ou la nouvelle Héloïse* (1761), another study of high sentiment; of Smollett's last novel, *Humphry Clinker* (1771), where it is used for an episodic novel of comic adventures across the island of Great Britain; for Goethe's *Werther* (1774), on a love unrequited to the point of suicide – a book translated four times into English before the end of the century, and three times into French; and Laclos's *Les liaisons dangereuses* (1782), a scandalous novel of seduction. Its prestige, then, is an unquestioned fact of that half-century. Though it may not have outnumbered the older form of the memoir-novel in the years between 1740 and 1790, either in French or in English, it plainly outdistanced it in experimental verve and notoriety. Fielding despised it, and never attempted it outside parody, but it is significant that Smollett moved towards it in his last and finest fiction, and that Fanny Burney wrote her first and very successful novel *Evelina* in 1778 in that form. The reign of the letter-novel, though short, was brilliant and highly acclaimed. Miss Burney received an appointment at the court of George III, Marie Antoinette kept a copy of *Les liaisons dangereuses*, plain bound, on her shelves, and Napoleon took a copy of *Werther* with him, as Goethe boasted, on his campaigns.

The two potent elements in the form, it has been suggested, are its impressive instancy and its approach to psychological truth, even to the stream of consciousness. Neither, for the eighteenth century, looked like unmixed blessings. Fielding derided, on both technical and moral grounds, reports seemingly written by characters within minutes or hours of the events they describe: 'Odsbobs! I hear him just coming in at the door. You see I write in the present tense . . . Well, he is in bed between us . . .', his Shamela writes to a confidante (letter vi). The novelist abandons the dignity of epic distance, as well as plausibility, when he speaks only in the pretended voices of his puppets; and *Joseph Andrews*, *Tom Jones* and *Amelia* are all attempts to restore that dignity, as comic or sentimental prose epics about contemporary England.

As for psychological realism, to speak anachronistically – it is a phrase the eighteenth century would not have understood – it offered something that could be seen as all too exciting at times, and exciting even to the point of indecency. The individual psyche could not in that age enjoy the status it holds in the twentieth century, and it must be admitted that the moral world of the letter-novel is often a hothouse of passion. The usual defence could be offered: that such instances were offered as a warning. Richardson, who saw himself as offering manuals of moral guidance to an age all too unlikely to spend its leisure in reading Scripture or *The Pilgrim's Progress*, never confused sincerity of response with virtue, and earned the moral approbation of a judge as severe as Samuel Johnson. For Rousseau that approbation might have been less apt, though Julie defends her new-found virtue as a married woman to the end of *La Nouvelle Héloïse*; and in Laclos, though *Les Liaisons dangereuses* ends with the direst punishment of the villains, the reader has by then been plunged into a perilous world of sexual licence and even sexual experiment. Even Richardson's Clarissa, who refuses marriage after being raped and dies in an edifying religious ecstasy, plainly indulges her mind in interdicted themes, on grounds however highminded; and the repentance of Lovelace, the rake who has so deeply offended her, does little to redeem the work from the charge of gloating.

In all these novels, decorum and morality are almost at one; right conduct is scarcely, if at all, to be distinguished from good manners, or good manners from pure thoughts. The letter-novel, to the end of its great century, remains a manual for manners: it can be a model of how letters are properly to be written, of how life is properly to be lived. Even the movement from *toi* to *vous*, in the *Lettres portugaises*, at the moment when the heroine realises that her lover never means to return to her, signalises a sense of how high sentiment is to be fittingly translated into decorous speech.

The ensuing century was to be less obsessed with decorum than this, and less certain that manners and morals are one. Trollope in his *Autobiography* (1883) tells how surprised he was to come upon a bundle of real love letters written by his mother to his father in 1809, and how little they resembled the slangy letters written by girls in the 1870s. Real as they were, they reminded him of a novel by Richardson or Fanny Burney: 'What girl now studies the words with which she shall address her lover, or seeks to charm him with grace of diction?' (ch. 2). All this helps to explain why Richardson and his successors influenced Henry James, Joyce and Virginia Woolf so little. The letter-novel came to look too frail a craft for the cargo it had come to bear. A comedy of manners one can understand: a tragedy of manners, for the Victorians and after, sounds like an almost impossible paradox of form.

★

At the height of its vogue, the conventions governing the epistolary mode were elaborate though shifting. Richardson retains the fiction of being an 'editor' rather than an author in all his three novels. *Pamela* calls itself 'a narrative which has its foundation in truth and nature' on its title-page, though the last two words were omitted in later editions; and *Clarissa*, eight years later, describes itself as 'published by the editor of *Pamela*'; *Grandison*, six years after that, as 'published from the originals by the editor of *Pamela* and *Clarissa*'. The pretence is in some degree maintained in the text. Richardson is not an author much famed for irony, but the preface to *Pamela* ends with a sly remark that 'an editor may reasonably be supposed to judge with an impartiality which is rarely to be met with in an author towards his own works'. But he thinks it beneath him to invent a story to explain in what cupboard or oak chest the letters were found: 'How such remarkable collections of private letters fell into his hands', he remarks in the preface to *Grandison*, 'he hopes the reader will not think it very necessary to enquire'. His own reflections on the matter suggest a balance that is less delicate than precarious. In a letter to William Warburton in April 1748, on *Clarissa*, he makes this exacting demand upon his more intelligent readers:

I could wish that the *air* of genuineness had been kept up, tho' I want not the letters to be *thought* genuine: only so far kept up, I mean, as that they should not prefatically be owned *not* to be genuine: and this for fear of weakening their influence where any of them are aimed to be exemplary; as well as to avoid hurting that kind of historical faith which fiction itself is generally read with, though we know it to be fiction.

The demand is refined to a point of impossibility; and it is based on an archaic assumption that a reader can only be edified by events he supposes to have actually occurred. Not many readers of *Clarissa*, and perhaps not even Warburton, can have satisfied all Richardson's conditions at once.

As the letter-novel evolves towards Rousseau, Fanny Burney and Laclos, these demands are loosened. No reader of *Evelina* or of *Les Liaisons dangereuses*, unless the most innocent, can have supposed those letters to have been real: Richardson's demand had proved too unstable to persist. Indeed *Evelina* is explicitly presented as a novel, with a foreword in which Fanny Burney begs the indulgence of the monthly reviewers, and a timid preface suggesting that the name of novelist has been rescued from the charge of depravity by such worthy exponents as Rousseau, Johnson, Marivaux, Fielding, Richardson and Smollett; though she ends by calling herself the 'editor' of the letters that comprise the book – a remark that looks like the wings of an emu.

★

Like the memoir, the letter bears within it restrictions characteristic of itself. Correspondents cannot reasonably be expected to write dialogue at great length, though in some eighteenth-century letter-novels they implausibly do. Nor can they be expected to write letters to one another if they live in the same house, unless some special circumstances apply – such as the tyranny of a parent or guardian. For this reason, no doubt, Pamela rarely writes to her master Mr B., whose attempt upon her virtue occurs under his own roof. Such lengthy exchanges none the less occur in *La Nouvelle Héloïse*. Characters may be confined by illness, after all, or locked away by parents, or eager to commit themselves more formally than by word of mouth.

Another restriction, for so long as it is accepted as one, relates to the number of correspondents. Since no literary terms are widely accepted here, I shall use a hodgepodge of musical ones. We might call a novel consisting of letters from one hand a monody, from two a duo, and from many a polyphony. Broadly speaking, the evolution of the letter-novel is from monody towards polyphony, though it is an unsteady one. The *Lettres portugaises* are an instance of seventeenth-century monody, being entirely written as by a nun to her departed lover. In *Pamela*, some seventy years later, there are six correspondents, which sounds impressively polyphonic; but the heroine's letters amount to nine-tenths of the whole, and Mr B. is allowed only two letters. (On the other hand, Pamela sometimes copies out the letters of others.) But *Clarissa* is monumentally and influentially polyphonic, with twenty-seven correspondents: Clarissa and Lovelace each accounting for about one-third of the novel. The predominance shifts from her letters to his, with Mr Belford, Lovelace's virtuous and reproachful confidant, dominating the tragic close. And Yet *Werther*, a quarter-century later, is almost entirely seen through the mind of its hero.

The limits of the epistolary, however, are subject to tolerances. One concerns the diary or journal. Like the memoir, the letter-novel can naturally encompass portions of diaries, especially if letters recount events day by day, as *Pamela* and *Werther* do. A diary, so to speak, is a letter written to oneself. There is, what is more, an interesting intermediate territory between the memoir and the letter, where lines are hard to draw. John Cleland's *Fanny Hill* (1748), for example, represents two long self-justifying letters on her scandalous career written to another woman, so that it amounts to a memoir in the form of letters. Marivaux's *La Vie de Marianne* and Diderot's *La Religieuse* occupy points in this intermediate territory. Other mixtures preserve the identity of the individual parts: Mary Shelley's *Frankenstein* (1818) begins and ends with Robert Walton's letter to his sister, telling of his friend Count Frankenstein, an idealistic young scientist; Frankenstein then recounts in a memoir how he unintentionally created a monster; and within that memoir is another, in which the monster tells his own bitter story of the world's rejection, so that the novel amounts to a memoir within a memoir within a letter, fitted like Chinese boxes.

★

The decline of the letter-novel is to be felt in the 1790s, and instances in English since 1800 are only occasional. Maria Edgeworth wrote fictional letters before the end of the century, but her *Leonora* (1806), a story of husband, wife and mistress in the sentimental manner of *Werther*, is among her weakest performances. Jane Austen, who was some seven years younger, experimented, too, in letters in the 1790s, as her juvenilia reveal, and there is evidence that *Sense and Sensibility* (1811), the first of her six novels to appear, was once drafted in epistolary form before she converted it into the third person. And Scott's *Redgauntlet* (1824) is epistolary for its first third: it begins with thirteen letters, and then falls back on the third person, on finding the form restrictive:

> A genuine correspondence of this kind (and Heaven forbid it should be in any respect sophisticated by interpolations of our own!) can seldom be found to contain all in which it is necessary to instruct the reader for his full comprehension of the story (ch. 1).

That heavy whimsy suggests a convention already moribund. It is certainly irksome.

The decline, however, proved a long one, and a number of Victorians dallied with epistolary forms in fiction. Anne Brontë's *Tenant of Wildfell Hall* (1848) is technically a letter-novel, though most of it consists of a long diary inserted into a letter. The first novel written by her sister Charlotte, *The Professor* (1857), begins with the implausible device of the hero happening upon a copy of a letter written years ago, and by himself, to a friend long since gone abroad, and this comprises the first chapter; the rest of the novel continues as a recollection in the first person. Charlotte had already toyed with the epistolary in *The Duke of Zamorna*, an Angrian romance written in 1838, where the opening and concluding chapters are dominated by letters. Technically considered, then, the fictions of the Brontës are perceptibly linked to the memoirs and letters of the preceding century, though floating free of them.

The epistolary cannot be called a vogue for the mid-Victorians. Dickens, Thackeray and Trollope never attempted letter-novels, though letters can be crucial to their plots, especially Trollope's. But Swinburne wrote his first novel, *A Year's Letters*, in the epistolary fashion in 1862; it remained unpublished till 1877, when it appeared expurgated in a journal, finally appearing in 1905 as *Love's Cross Currents*. Being devoted to a variety of sexual experiences, including flagellation, its archaic form perhaps embodies a Victorian sentiment concerning the wider licences of eighteenth-century life. And Henry James, as a young novelist, proposed to himself in his notes for January 1879 'a story told in letters written alternately by a mother and her daughter, and giving totally different accounts of the same situation', which emerged as 'A Bundle of Letters'. He was later to attempt the form in 'The Point of View'. Since the abiding charm of the letter-novel, especially in its advanced or polyphonic form, lies in its variety of views, it is odd James used it so rarely, and George Eliot and Conrad hardly at all.

By the twentieth century, the epistolary mode is a matter for self-conscious revival, and that only rarely. E. M. Forster's *Howards End* (1910) begins in a disarmingly casual style, 'One may as well begin with Helen's letters to her sister', and does so, with two letters to Margaret announcing Helen's engagement to a young man she has met on holiday in Germany; whereupon the narration slides off naturally into the third person, Forster donning what elsewhere he calls the novelist's 'cap of invisibility'. *The Nature of a Crime* (1924), a collaboration between Conrad and Ford Madox Ford, consists of a bundle of letters from a man to a married woman who has gone abroad concerning his relations with her and her husband; but they were not, apparently, sent one by one. Henry Green's first novel, *Blindness* (1926), begins with a long diary and ends with a short letter, as if the novel were sandwiched between the traditional forms of the memoir and the epistolary; and Guido Piovene's *Lettere di una novizia* (1941) is an epistolary account of a young woman about to be a nun, and her relations with her mother. Saul Bellow's *Herzog* (1964), though hardly a letter-novel, embodies an insane correspondence, one-sided only, by which the hero admonishes famous and powerful figures around the world as well as his own acquaintances. Christopher Isherwood's *A Meeting by the River* (1967), on the other hand, is a clear and genuine instance, and an historical sport: a novel radically epistolary, interspersed with a diary in the eighteenth-century manner, but utterly twentieth-century in its style and theme. The story is sustained without technical strain: a telling little reminder that a form awaits its master, whenever the master calls.

★

But for two centuries since Fanny Burney the letter-novel has failed to provide an abiding form for any eminent novelist in English. In practical terms, the twentieth-century novelist commonly feels he has to choose between 'I' and 'he', and 'he' has easily predominated. Omniscience has won. Indeed, the tradition of omniscient narration which has dominated the novel since 1800 by now looks as a prevailing form unshakeable.

A little bridge, however, leads into it from the memoir and the letter. It may be called the 'Bridge of the Observer-Narrator': a first-person form where the story is told by a minor character who sees, hears and interprets, often in a manner only doubtfully reliable, the behaviour of the principals, as in *Paul et Virginie* and *Castle Rackrent*. The triumph of omniscience has not meant that the novelist knows everything about what his creatures are, or everything about what they think and do. It has meant that, as their creator, he has held himself entitled to do so: to spy upon their doings, even when alone; to interpret motive as well as action; and to enter their secret souls and unspoken, even unconscious, reflections. All that is a prevailing assumption in nineteenth-century fiction and since, if not entirely a universal one.

In the first two decades of the twentieth century comes a step forward which is also a step back. The stream-of-consciousness novel that arose with Proust, Joyce and Dorothy Richardson represents, on one view, the last victory for omniscience since it claims to see the whole of a mind. But it can also be seen as the first retreat. To see the world predominantly out of a single mind, as in Joyce's *Portrait of the Artist as a Young Man*, or out of several, as in his *Ulysses*, is perhaps not to see the world at all, and certainly not to see it steadily or whole. The mind of a character is less plausibly all-seeing than that of a novelist. That is why it is hard to answer the question: is stream of consciousness a mark of an advance in omniscient confidence, or a withdrawal? The mind of a character is not necessarily all-revealing. When Joyce's *Ulysses* appeared, even the modernist reaction was sceptical. As Virginia Woolf reports in her diary (26 September 1922), T. S. Eliot's private view was less enthusiastic than his public one: 'This new method of giving the psychology proves to my mind that it doesn't work. It doesn't tell as much as some casual glance from outside often tells'; and Virginia Woolf, agreeing with him, added that she preferred *Pendennis*.

The international coincidence of events, for all that, is evidently more than a coincidence, and plainly signifies the next step that fiction had to take: Proust's *A la recherche* began to appear in 1913,

Joyce's *Portrait* in 1914, in its serial form, and Dorothy Richardson's twelve-part *Pilgrimage* in 1915. They were composed independently of one another, in their beginnings, but in a manner highly dependent of that stage in its evolution which the novel by 1900 had everywhere reached. At that moment, early in the new century, omniscience took stock of itself, as if asking to be forgiven for some excess of confidence and of zeal.

★

The beginnings of narrative omniscience in the novel are harder to date, and may be more English than French. It is perhaps here, in the most durable of all fictional conventions of the modern world, that the English novel most convincingly shakes off the charge of being parasitic upon other cultures. Fielding had staked a claim to epic omniscience in the 1740s, long before any French novelist of similar celebrity – though the French *nouvelle* and *conte* were already practising it. And Smollett, who managed to try everything available, employed it in *Peregrine Pickle* (1751) by claiming the classical warrant of satire.

But its continuous life is harder to date at its source. On one interpretation, after all, it amounted to a revival of claims once readily accepted in epics and romances, so that fictional omniscience might better be seen as a revival of an ancient claim than as the invention of a modern one. To that extent, Fielding's appeal (and Smollett's) to Greek and Latin precedents makes good history. But it was not an appeal that succeeded at once. Jane Austen finally composed all her six novels in this manner, to appear between 1811 and 1818, and may perhaps be seen as the first European master in that continuous life; Scott, who began to publish novels in 1814, is perhaps the second. The first French masters are Balzac and Stendhal, both followers of Scott: *Les Chouans* of Balzac appeared in 1829, Stendhal's *Le Rouge et le noir* in the year after. In this respect, then, the great names of the French *roman* lag a generation behind the English; and the vogue of Scott, which stretched across the nineteenth century through France and Germany into the Russia of Tolstoy, guaranteed that the debt to the novel in English was conscious and avowed.

From the all-seeing eye of the novelist, henceforth, character cannot escape. It is apt that the limitless claims of the novel in the last century to reveal and instruct should be matched by a technique that accepted, in principle, no limits to knowledge. An individual novelist might still be ignorant in diverse ways, including ways that affect his grasp of a chosen field. But that is personal deficiency, not a limit inherent in the form. The novel since 1800 has claimed to see more than the human heart. It has seen civilisations as a whole, and the differences between them, as in Scott, Tolstoy and Forster; past ages, and how they differ from the present, as in Scott, Manzoni and Flaubert; the recent past, as in Dickens, Thackeray and George Eliot; and above all the present, as in Jane Austen and Trollope, or what he called 'The Way We Live Now'; how to live it better, or at the worst easier.

These claims are still admitted by novelists, and exploited by them, however much it may be fashionable for critics to cavil. The novelist still wants to see the whole of his theme, and to reveal grand distinctions like those that divide whole nations. 'One of these differences we can take in at a glance', writes David Lodge at the start of *Changing Places* (1975), as he watches his two heroes, one British and the other American, as they cross by air in mid-Atlantic – to exchange wives, in the event, as well as jobs; and his glance, as he imagines it, is 'from our privileged narrative altitude – higher than that of any jet'. Omniscience is indeed higher than any jet. But then, since the novelist has made his creatures, he may persuasively claim to know them too.

NOTE

1. Robert Adams Day, *Told in Letters: Epistolary Fiction before Richardson* (Ann Arbor; 1966) p. 2. See also Vivienne Mylne, 'Letter-novels', in her *Eighteenth-century French Novel* (Manchester: 1965) pp. 144–55.

4 *Dialogue*

Dialogue, as everyone now thinks, enlivens a novel. In libraries and bookshops, aspiring readers may be seen turning the pages, confident they can tell at a glance whether dialogue predominates, and whether in a brisk and animated way. It now represents the most important fact one can easily discover about a novel without actually reading it.

The evolution of dialogue has been largely an acceptance of that popular taste. It is a history, by and large, of increasing frequency and brevity, moving away from the great blocks of set speeches common in the seventeenth-century romance, still subject in some degree to the rules of classical rhetoric, towards the quick to-and-fro favoured by many readers since the novel came of age. A novel containing no dialogue at all, like Marguerite Yourcenar's *Mémoires d'Hadrien* (1951), is a notable rarity in the present century.

Growing both brisker and more predominant, and detaching itself typographically from its enveloping tissue of narrative prose, dialogue has evolved over three centuries towards the buoyancy of such extreme exploitation as P. G. Wodehouse's, where a speech can be as brief as one or two words, and where the exchanges are set out on the page as a captivating trickle, to draw the reader in and propel the story forward at the same time.

> I reached out a hand from under the blankets, and rang the bell for Jeeves.
> 'Good evening, Jeeves.'
> 'Good morning, sir.'
> This surprised me.
> 'Is it morning?'
> 'Yes, sir.'

So opens *The Code of the Woosters* (1938): a near-dramatic technique where the narrative comment, though minimal ('This surprised me'), is still sufficient as a frame for dialogue. It is a technique evolved out of long experience and a dozen generations of novelists. That it took so long to evolve is a measure of the traditional inhibitions against allowing dialogue so large an operational role in works which, after all, are not designed for theatre.

In this chapter I shall consider the place of dialogue within narrative, the nature of those traditional inhibitions, and the manner of their slow decline and fall.

★

The texture of fiction may be usefully divided into seven modes, though in practice they are not entirely self-exclusive, and cannot hope to exhaust the possibilities. (For this purpose I shall choose illustrations from the beginnings of novels, more often than not, to reduce the distortion of quoting out of context.)

1. *Authorial voice*, where the author speaks in his own person, offering an opinion or a view directly rather than through a character. Samuel Johnson's *Rasselas* (1759) begins: 'Ye who listen with credulity to the whispers of fancy, and pursue with eagerness the phantoms of hope . . . ; attend to the history of Rasselas. . . .' The passage is declarative rather than narrative, and it is Johnson himself who warns against credulous optimism.

2. *Plain narrative*, where one is told what happened. 'In the latter days of July in the year 185–', Trollope's *Barchester Towers* (1857) begins, 'a most important question was for ten days hourly asked in the cathedral city of Barchester, and answered every hour in various ways – Who was to be the new Bishop?'

3. *Coloured narrative*, where something which a character (or in the fullest instances, a narrator) supposed or thought is indicated in the third person. Much of Prévost's *Manon Lescaut* (1731) is like that, being told by the love-sick Des Grieux; or Conrad's *Heart of Darkness* (1902). Charlotte Brontë's *Jane Eyre* (1847) begins: 'There was no possibility of taking a walk that day' – a judgement on the weather which, as the ensuing sentences show, had been made, among others, by the odious Mrs Reed, guardian to Jane as a little girl.

4. *Free indirect speech* (*style indirect libre*), where the speech of a

character is embedded in the narrative, free of conjunctions, inverted commas and other indicators of direct speech such as 'he said'. This requires the mind and style of a character to have been already established, so that it can hardly open a novel. But Dickens, in a surprising turn, imitates the speech habits of Mr Gradgrind at the start of the second chapter of *Hard Times* (1854):

> Thomas Gradgrind, sir. A man of realities. A man of facts and calculations. A man who proceeds upon the principle that two and two are four, and nothing over, and who is not to be talked into allowing for anything over. Thomas Gradgrind, sir – peremptorily Thomas – Thomas Gradgrind. With a rule and a pair of scales, and the multiplication table always in his pocket, sir, ready to weigh and measure any parcel of human nature . . .

5. *Indirect speech*, or *oratio obliqua*. The opening of *Jane Eyre* offers an illustrative instance which the modern reader may fail to recognise because of the printer's use of inverted commas – common enough attendants of indirect speech until the later nineteenth century:

> Me, she had dispensed from joining the group, saying 'She regretted to be under the necessity of keeping me at a distance; but that until she heard from Bessie . . . that I was endeavouring in good earnest to acquire a more sociable and childlike disposition, . . . she really must exclude me from privileges intended only for contented, happy little children.'

6. *Direct speech, oratio recta,* or dialogue. Jane Eyre, the heroine, enters dialogue at this point for the first time: "What does Bessie say I have done?" I asked. . . .'

7. *Description,* usually of persons or places, where the time sequence of narrative is abandoned in favour of analysis. Dickens is fond of introducing a character in a whirl of tiny, highly visual details; here is Mr Turveydrop in *Bleak House* (1853):

> He was a fat old gentleman with a false complexion, false teeth, false whiskers, and a wig. He had a fur collar, and he had a padded breast to his coat . . . He was pinched in, and swelled out, and got up, and strapped down, as much as he could possibly bear. . . . (ch. 14)

The first and last of these seven modes, it will be noted, are non-narrative.

★

The evolution and growth of dialogue in the novel through the eighteenth and nineteenth centuries is largely a story of its progressive liberation from the remaining six of these elements. In the early novel, dialogue is often felt to be a privileged mode of discourse and one proper to drama rather than to novels – and so involving a daring or in-decorous mixture of *genres*: the reader expecting, even demanding, to be gently prepared for it. That inhibition was felt as late as Victorian fiction, though diminishingly. It explains the opening of *Jane Eyre*, which steps down from a coloured narrative (3) bordering on plain (2) – 'There was no possibility . . .' (it doubtless was raining hard, that day in Yorkshire), before entering free indirect speech (4) – 'Me, she had dispensed from joining the group . . .' – a phrase that may be close to what Mrs Reed said to Jane; and so into indirect speech (5) and finally direct speech (6), with Jane's first remark. This satisfies a traditional demand for hesitation in the use of dialogue. It also confers upon the heroine herself, who is only a little girl here, a narrative eminence which, as narrator, Jane vengefully denies to her harsh guardian and her spoiled companions.

The same descent into dialogue – or rather, in this case, a thought within inverted commas – can be watched in the opening of Lewis Carroll's *Alice in Wonderland* (1865) nearly twenty years later, though by now the movement is so fast as to be almost a blur:

> Alice was beginning to get very tired of sitting by her sister on the bank, and of having nothing to do: once or twice she had peeped into the book her sister was reading, but it had no pictures or conversations in it, 'and what is the use of a book,' thought Alice, 'without pictures or conversations?'

'It had no pictures . . .' is a brief element of free indirect style, and 'conversations' is Alice's childish word for dialogue. Long before 1865 it was an expectation of readers that dialogue should be spaced out as such on the page rather than run together within narrative, so that Alice is probably right to feel she can dislike a book without having read it.

Given that dialogue, in the early novel, needed to be gently introduced, the dialogue opening was exceptional in the nineteenth century and almost unknown in the eighteenth, though it is commonplace in the twentieth. It was in no way radical of Kingsley Amis to begin his first novel, *Lucky Jim* (1953), with a remark in mid-conversation from the hero's elderly and tedious superior, Professor Welch, leaving the story to catch up during the rest of the first chapter:

> 'They made a silly mistake, though,' the professor of history said, and his smile, as Dixon watched, gradually sank beneath the surface of his features at the memory. . . .

On the other hand, it must have looked astonishing at the opening of Sterne's *Sentimental Journey* (1768), which is perhaps the first European novel to begin with a remark of dialogue; but then Sterne's reputation for technical virtuosity was already established by *Tristram Shandy*, and the start of the *Sentimental Journey*, like the finish, may represent a sort of witty fracture, with something broken off at either end:

> – They order, said I, this matter better in France. –
> – You have been in France? said my gentleman, turning quick upon me with the most civil triumph in the world. . . .

to conclude:

> . . . So that when I stretch'd out my hand, I caught hold of the fille de chambre's

The *Sentimental Journey* has the double distinction then of being the first novel to begin with dialogue, and the first (and almost only) novel to end without punctuation. No eighteenth-century French novel of note begins in this way.

By the mid-nineteenth century, however, the instances have grown more numerous, at least in English. Susan Ferrier began *Marriage* (1818) with ' "Come hither, child," said the old Earl . . .'; Disraeli opened *Sybil* (1845) with an exchange of dialogue, and later *Lothair* (1870); and Dickens allowed it to himself once, and once only, in his fourteen novels, though the opening of *Hard Times* (1854) might better be described as an unanswered monologue, addressed by Mr Grad-grind to a schoolmaster:

> Now, what I want is, Facts. Teach these boys and girls nothing but Facts. . . .

All these cases must have looked odder in their day than they do now. The twentieth century feels this mode of opening to be normal: Thomas Mann used it for *Buddenbrooks* (1901), his first novel, and Ronald Furbank in his first three (1915–16). By the inter-war years it was unremarkable. But Ivy Compton-Burnett is perhaps the only notable novelist to begin all her mature fictions in this way.

★

The advance of dialogue was neither rapid nor continuous. Its very punctuation and arrangement on the page were for long uncertain, with numerous variations between individual printers, including italics for the spoken words, and even a dramatic arrangement with the speaker's name at the start of each speech – a form sometimes occurring even in letter-novels, as in Richardson's *Clarissa* (V, 26). It was only as late as the 1780s that French and English settled into something approaching their present conventions: the French opting for what they supposed a predominantly English form, or starting each speech with a dash, as in the opening of Sterne's *Sentimental Journey*; and the English adopting one version of the French system, or inverted commas. By 1800 the initiatory dash was to look characteris-tic of French fiction and inverted commas of the English; though Joyce, a cosmopolitan writing in Trieste and Paris, was to prefer the French dash in his handling of English dialogue. But Alice, if she had lived a hundred years earlier, might not have felt so certain after a glance at her sister's book that it contained no conversations, since the convention of starting each speech with a new line was not regularly established before 1800; and speeches, in any case, could be para-graph long in eighteenth-century fiction, and even more.

The growth of dialogue as a propellent of narrative was unsteady. Richardson, like other eighteenth-century novelists, often handles scenes in which the story concerns shifting relations between charac-ters, and where those shifts are marked by dialogue and little else: what he said to her, and what she said to him. But the proportion of dialogue is often less, for all that, than it would have been a century or two later, with a greater prominence to such intermediate forms as indirect speech. Dickens uses dialogue with full power, and as a principal mode of story-telling, as early as his first novel, *The Pickwick Papers* (1836–7); but he seems to prefer it for situations of comedy and even farce, and some of his later novels are more discursive than his first. George Eliot, whose first novel appeared in 1859, uses it less, and less adroitly, as befits an unremittingly analytical mind; and though Henry James moved strongly towards it in the 1890s, in his period of obsession with the theatre, and encouraged *The Awkward Age* (1899) to approach dramatic form in its emphasis upon dialogue, he moved after 1900 into a less theatrical and less lively mode, where coloured narrative has a notable place. And yet the growth of dialogue over the centuries, for all these checks, strikes one as essentially irresistible.

The sources of the inhibition against dialogue are curious to consider. One was vulgarity: polite readers continued to prefer a correct standard of speech, and even to insist on it. That is why 'common' speech needs to be excused, as Defoe excuses Moll Flanders's, though Challe had already used some exceptionally realistic exchanges in the frame-story for his *Les Illustres Françoises* (1713), and Marivaux was to be scolded by his critics for a low-life quarrel in *La Vie de Marianne* (1731–41). Dialect, or a regional version of the vulgar, only rarely enters the English novel before 1800, apart from a few stagey Scots, Irishmen and the like; and even where it enters powerfully, as in the Yorkshire characters of the Brontë sisters, or in West Country speech with Hardy, it is modified in order not to baffle or repel polite taste. To this day it remains a question whether a reader wants idiosyncrasies of speech, whether social, regional or merely personal, to be forced continually upon his attention. The effort can be fatiguing even when the effect is not repulsive. It is also faintly implausible, for some. The great fault of Fanny Burney's *Cecilia* (1782), Horace Walpole remarked acutely in a letter, is that she is

. . . so afraid of not making all her *dramatis personæ* set in character, that she never lets them say a syllable but what is to mark their character, which is very unnatural; at least in the present state of things, in which people are always aiming to disguise their ruling passions, and rather affect opposite qualities than hang out their propensities. (1 October 1782)

Since many people are as skilled in disguising their regional origins as their oddities of character, it might well be argued that it is absurd for a novelist to parade them. Far from being a realistic element, oddities of speech can all too easily look implausible and unreal. They can certainly tire.

Another source of suspicion, if not hostility, relates to the origins of the novel, real or imagined, in classical epic and seventeenth-century romance. Such works obey certain rules of literary decorum. They are not, as drama is, radically based on dialogue. They rarely allow brisk exchanges of speeches, as opposed to long set speeches, to propel the narrative forward, but prefer such exchanges to work as a decorative or illustrative element, just as they preserve a decorum of style within speeches. English fiction, which was often less confinedly aristocratic than French in the eighteenth century, was breaking free of these inhibitions as early as Defoe. Smollett, a radical liberator in his use of dialogue, even interested himself in its psychological oddities, long before Chekhov or Harold Pinter, and a little before Sterne's Uncle Toby; and he remarks in a letter on the queer habit some people have of 'answering from the purpose', or replying in a manner not required by the question, instancing someone who, on being asked if he had ever known an honester fellow than a certain acquaintance, replied: 'By God, I was at his mother's burial' (1 March 1754). That is a real intuition of how mind works, or fails to work. But it requires a certain indifference to decorum to dare to use it.

★

The technical progress of fiction in the eighteenth century, nowhere so marked as in dialogue, lies in a growing confidence in itself and a gradual forgetting of its roots. By the nineteenth, the cry is all for liveliness. Trollope recommended that a speech should rarely exceed a dozen words. The printed page, after all, has to work hard to make good the loss of intonation that speech possesses in life and in the theatre, and much that sounds lively in the mouth looks like cold turkey on the page.

The best trick here, and the hardest, is to write speeches that force a highly marked intonation upon the reader's mind. Richardson and Smollett have that enviable gift. Jane Austen, for whom Richardson was a favourite author, uses dialogue for witty concentrates of language, and often triumphs by economy. 'Can he be a sensible man, sir?' Elizabeth Bennet asks of her father, on receiving Mr Collins's letter in *Pride and Prejudice* (1813), to which Mr Bennet replies composedly: 'No, my dear; I think not. I have great hopes of finding him quite the reverse' (ch. 13). Such sentences are a gift to the actor's ear, even in the least histrionic of readers: they can only sound in one way, and that as the novelist meant them to sound.

It is not surprising, then, if the taste for dialogue grows. Scott recognised that it could make things less flat. 'You blame me for introducing dialogue', he wrote to his publisher Ballantyne in the winter of 1814–15, on *Guy Mannering* (1815), 'but you [are] not aware that the incidents which must be known would be flatter in the mouth of the author himself than in those of the actors.' Odd that a novelist should ever have needed to give that advice to a publisher; for the Victorians, it was ordinarily a matter of advice from publisher to novelist. But Scott, though not continuously adept in applying the principle, was already learning it. Dialogue disciplines a novelist into brevity and enlivens his page to the eye of a reader. It is the wine of Victorian fiction. That is something Henry James sometimes needed to be told.

One has seen good solid slices of fiction, well endued one might surely have thought with the easiest of lubrications, deplored by editor and publisher as positively not, for the general gullet known to *them*, made adequately 'slick'.

'Dialogue, always dialogue,' I had heard from far back to hear them mostly cry: 'We can't have too much of it, and no excess of it . . .' This wisdom had always been in one's ears,

he complained in a preface to *The Awkward Age*, protesting that the English, for all their love of dramatic speech, will not buy the texts of plays they admire, as Parisians do. His later fiction, especially, after 1900, contrasts a highly sophisticated prose of objective or coloured narrative with startlingly colloquial dialogue, tricked out with circumlocutions in place of 'he said' and 'she said', which he had come to feel were impossibly commonplace. This is by now among the most easily mimicked of Jamesian mannerisms – 'he risked', 'she ventured', and the like. In his later fiction it works towards a larger effect: an extreme dissimilation between the novelist's own mannered voice, on the one hand, and the highly colloquial remarks of his characters; all serving to enhance a reader's sense of the creator's superior intelligence over his fallen creatures.

By the mid-twentieth century, there is no limit to the work that dialogue can be set by the novelist to do. Though its role can still be relatively minor, it rarely looks as minor as it did before Smollett and Sterne made of it a chief motive force in story-telling. It can be used as a modest illustrative device; or, as in the novels of Ivy Compton-Burnett, it can fill the plot until it usurps the ordinary functions of narrative prose. If dialogue is the essence of drama, then a novel can now be as dramatic or as undramatic as the novelist pleases. But it now seems irreversibly true that, whatever pleases the novelist, the modern reader will always ask for more dialogue: 'We can't have too much of it, and no excess of it. . . .'

5 *Titles and Devices*

A novel looks like a novel, more often than not. By what devices is it recognised? In this chapter I shall move briskly through books from start to finish, beginning with the title-page.

★

TITLES

Early novels often signal on their title-pages the literary kind to which they belong. A memoir-novel is often entitled a 'history'; and in the English of the seventeenth and eighteenth centuries, the word can mean a story, whether true or fictional, as '*histoire*' still does in French. But it often implies a claim to truth, and confusions can be deliberate here. In his preface to *Roxana* (1724), Defoe called his novel 'not a story, but a history', since its foundation was 'laid in truth of fact'. Another common term here is 'life', meaning biography. 'Romance' and 'novel', unlike 'history', can only refer to fictions; but 'novel', which is recorded in English as the name of a literary form as early as the 1560s, and scornfully mentioned by Milton in his divorce pamphlets in the 1640s ('no mere amatorious novel'), is far less common in titles before 1800 than 'history', which has the ambiguous dignity of confounding fact and fable.

In memoir-titles, 'life' may be enlarged with such appropriate terms as 'adventures' and 'death', even though no hero can describe his own decease. Defoe's title for *Robinson Crusoe* (1719) begins: *The Life and Strange Surprizing Adventures of Robinson Crusoe of York, Mariner, written by himself* . . . ; and its sequel, in the same year, as *The Farther Adventures* . . . In letter-novels titles are more often descriptive, as in the anonymous *Passionate Love-letters between a Polish Princess and a Certain Chevalier* (1719); or a balance of name and description, like

51

Richardson's *Pamela: or Virtue Rewarded* (1740). That balance can be reversed, of course – but in that case the novel may easily become known by its subtitle rather than its title, or simply by the hero's name: who now thinks of John Cleland's pornographic masterpiece, *Memoirs of a Woman of Pleasure* (1748), as anything except as *Fanny Hill*? But in one curious instance a descriptive subtitle has pushed out the main title, itself the name of the heroine, in public esteem: Rousseau's *Julie: ou la nouvelle Héloïse* (1761) is now universally known by its subtitle, which elegantly refers the reader to a famous medieval tale of frustrated love. No one seems to call it *Julie*, and few will regret Rousseau's first idea for a title, *Lettres de deux amants*, which appeared in the earliest editions.

Before 1800, at least, and especially in novels of scale and pretension, subtitles are more common than not, and the fashion did not fade until Victorian times. Of Dickens's fourteen novels, the first three (1836–9) are equipped with them; but they vanish from his later title-pages, which are more sparsely named, *Bleak House* being the entire title of that novel as it appeared in 1853. Dickens's last pastiche of the long eighteenth-century title, equipped even with a subtitle that begins '*comprising . . .*', is *Martin Chuzzlewit* (1844), where the whole title is sixty-nine words long, and laughably verbose: . . . *with an historical record of what he did, and what he didn't. . . .* But the parody is just, after all, and scarcely overdrawn. *Crusoe* had a title of sixty-eight words, *Moll Flanders* sixty-nine: both of them amounting to summaries of entire plots, presumably as enticement to the reader. Moll, for example, is described on her title-page as . . . *twelve year a whore, five times a wife (whereof once to her own brother), twelve year a thief, eight year a transported felon in Virginia, at last grew rich, liv'd honest, and died a penitent* . . . The eighteenth-century reader, and especially early in that century, was supposed to want guarantees before he borrowed or bought.

Richardson's titles are a little shorter, and indicate their epistolary form by the use of 'editor'; they are not narrative titles, like Defoe's, but moral in content. The forty-one-word title of *Clarissa* (1748), for example, identifies the chief point of edification as . . . *particularly shewing the distress that may attend the misconduct both of parents and children in relation to marriage. . . .* Fielding's titles are much shorter, and neither narrative nor moral: a brevity that befits his claim to epic status. That of *Tom Jones* is only seven words long – 'The history of Tom Jones, a foundling' – and though *Joseph Andrews*, seven years earlier, had been allowed a much longer title, much of it is occupied with identifying its literary source: '. . . written in imitation of the manner of Cervantes, author of Don Quixote. . . ' . Smollett's titles, too, are modest in length; and Sterne, though he parodies most of the elements of the memoir-novel in his masterpiece, does not imitate its garrulous title-page, which is content with *The life and opinions of Tristram Shandy, gentleman.*

By the next century, a wordy title is necessarily parody, and the age can even admit single-word titles like Maria Edgeworth's *Belinda* (1801) and *Patronage* (1814) – the one a name, the other a theme; while Jane Austen's titles are always short, and always without subtitles. Scott can allow himself subtitles, on occasion, but briefly, and his play with eighteenth-century formularies is largely confined to prefaces and postscripts by such imaginary bores as Captain Clutterbuck and Dr Dryasdust – or by 'the author of Waverley' himself. This disdain for titular elaboration early in the nineteenth century helps to confirm the judgement that, of all the great novelists of his age, Dickens has the liveliest consciousness of the fictional techniques of the preceding century, and it is a consciousness not merely derisive: his use of 'history', after all, in the title of *David Copperfield* (1850) draws a mind-stretching contrast between the modern novel of mind and its remote predecessors in Fielding and Smollett.

But few novelists achieve or even seek a totally characteristic style in their titles. Those of Raymond Chandler's eight Marlowe novels, it has been ingeniously suggested, were alphabetical, if one omits the definite article; but this could be chance. Graham Greene, since he began with *The Man Within* in 1929, has usually preferred phrases such as *Brighton Rock* (1938) or *The Human Factor* (1978) – a thirtyish style, especially for thrillers; and Henry Green was fond of single words, like *Living* (1929) and *Loving* (1945). But only Ivy Compton-Burnett, perhaps, has achieved anything approaching consistency, almost always insisting on an 'and' to link nouns that are not proper names. Over a long life her novels appeared every two years in uneven years, apart from a minor dislocation occasioned by the Second World War, until *The Last and the First* (1971), her last novel, appeared a symbolic two years after her death.

★

Broadly speaking, there are three kinds of titles for novels:

1. The name of a hero or heroine, such as *Tom Jones* or *Lucky Jim*, once commonly accompanied by a generic term such as 'memoirs' or

'history' – an accompaniment that largely drops away in the nineteenth century; or a phrase descriptive of a person or persons, such as *The English Lovers* (1661–2) or Dickens's *Our Mutual Friend* (1865).

Names, being commonly more memorable than descriptions, are inclined to predominate over them. Herman Melville's most famous novel appeared first under a descriptive title, *The Whale*, in London in October 1851, but only because Melville's request for a change reached his British publisher too late. It appeared as *Moby Dick: or the Whale* next month, in New York.

2. The name of a place or building, such as Horace Walpole's *Castle of Otranto* (1765), the first known instance. This remains rare throughout the rest of that century, outside Gothic novels, of which Walpole is a pioneer; though there were precedents in old romance, such as Sidney's *Arcadia* (1590). But it increases in the nineteenth century and since: Jane Austen's *Mansfield Park* (1814), Scott's *Monastery* (1820), Stendhal's *La Chartreuse de Parme* (1839) – though there the Italian charterhouse is only mentioned on the last page – Dickens's *Old Curiosity Shop* (1841), E. M. Forster's *Howards End* (1910).

Taken as a whole, that growth is evidently linked to a developing sense of region and locality in fiction, and the symbolic value of place. It was something of a hallmark of Gothic novels throughout the last third of the eighteenth century – hence Jane Austen's *Northanger Abbey* (1818), which was first called *Miss Catherine*, her parody of that school. The French, when they borrowed the Gothic, seem to have felt this even more strongly than the English, and Ann Radcliffe's *A Romance of the Forest* (1791) was translated as *La Forêt: ou l'abbaye de Saint-Clair* (1794).

Otranto is a fanciful instance of the new interest in place; *Wuthering Heights* a down-to-earth one. By the mid-nineteenth century titles of place have shifted from the Gothic to the regional. It is odd, then, that Thomas Hardy, that supremely regional novelist, does not favour titles in this form, though he gives the name of Wessex to his tales and poems, and to his first great collection of fiction, the *Wessex Novels* of 1895–6.

3. An abstraction or saying, whether word, phrase or sentence. This is out of question for the earliest novelists of note, whether in French or in English, though there are minor instances before 1750; but the fashion grows. Eliza Haywood's *Love in Excess: or the Fatal*

Enquiry (1719), a highly successful melodramatic romance, is among the earliest, in title and subtitle – both of them resembling titles for plays, which she also wrote; and two *contes* of Voisenon, *Il eut raison* and *Il eut tort*, both of 1750, show a new syntactical freedom, though it is unlikely Trollope had heard of either when he wrote *He Knew He Was Right* (1869).

This is a species of title that grew common shortly before the Victorians. Jane Austen employs it in three of her six novels – *Sense and Sensibility*, *Pride and Prejudice* and *Persuasion*, all abstractions, and two of them in couples – a formula implying a moral contrast between characters already in vogue before 1800. (A philosopher once suggested that *Emma* might be illuminatingly re-entitled as *Influence and Interference*, and *Mansfield Park* as *Solicitude*.)[1] Scott does not use such titles, however, preferring names, and Dickens uses it only occasionally: *Hard Times, for Our Times* (1854) is a curious expansion of a familiar phrase, and *Great Expectations* (1860) a common expression for someone expecting a legacy. Thackeray uses it in the first of his novels to appear, *Vanity Fair* (1848), a phrase drawn from Bunyan, but never afterwards. Other Victorians employ it abundantly, even extravagantly: Charles Reade in *It Is Never Too Late To Mend* (1856) and *The Cloister and the Hearth* (1861), where the two nouns are to be abstractly understood as referring to monastic and marital life; and Trollope sometimes allows himself eccentrically interrogative titles like *Can You Forgive Her?* (1864) – a misleading name for the first of his Palliser novels on parliamentary life – or *Is He Popenjoy?* (1878), a novel about the legitimacy of an heir. Perhaps the oddest of Victorian titles is Wilkie Collins's *I Say No* (1884), but by then the fashion for such oddities was already turning. Hardy, Gissing and Wells are usually less adventurous in the matter; Wells, indeed, in his social fiction resolutely conforms to an older tradition, as in *Kipps* (1905) and *The History of Mr Polly* (1910).

The experimental novel of the early twentieth century rarely brought its love of innovation to bear upon the title-page. Though novels tell stories, even when experimental, it is still exceptional for a title to represent an event, like Smollett's *The Expedition of Humphry Clinker* (1771), or Kafka's *Der Prozess* (1925), or Graham Greene's *The End of the Affair* (1951). The commonest single form for novel-titles in this century probably remains the name of a character, or a phrase descriptive of that character: *Mrs Dalloway*, *Herzog*, *A Word-child*. A proverbial title remains possible, like Forster's *Where Angels Fear To*

Tread or John Braine's *Room at the Top*, either of which would have done for a mid-Victorian novel. The nearest approach to innovation, and that a mild one, is to extend the saying or proverb into the field of literary allusion and quotation – commoner in English than in French, in all probability, though Proust does it: *The Sound and the Fury, Eyeless in Gaza, The Sun Also Rises*; but Hardy had been fond of this style as early as the 1870s, with *Under the Greenwood Tree*, a title as Shakespearean as Faulkner's.

A subtler species, harder to recognise and trace back to its roots, lies in the seemingly commonplace phrase that harbours a symbolic point. Scarron's *Le Roman comique* (1651–7) is almost a punning title, being at once comic and about *comédiens* or actors; Marmontel's *Contes moraux* (1761–5), as its preface explains, is a collection of tales about *moeurs* and *morale*, manners and morality, at the same time; and André Gide's *Symphonie pastorale* (1919) is told by a pastor and set in the country.

But a double significance is after all easy to grasp. What, by contrast, is one to make of Henry James's *The Wings of a Dove* (1902), which he first provisionally entitled *La Mourante* – or Forster's *Passage to India* (1924), or Iris Murdoch's *Under the Net* (1954)? Such titles perform nothing of the traditional task of providing the reader with information before he begins, and they stand at the remotest extreme from the title-pages of Defoe and Richardson. But they echo in the mind after reading, and even in the course of it: resonant phrases of shifting significance, that never seem to exhaust their fund of sense.

NAMES OF CHARACTERS

Since the names of characters often dominated the very titles of memoir-novels and letter-novels, they were of decisive significance in early fiction. It was an assumption, especially in comic works, that names should in some sense represent character or role. Aristotle, speaking of drama, remarks in the *Poetics* (ch. 9) that authors of tragedies keep the historical names of characters, whereas authors of comedies invent characteristic ones. Samuel Johnson in his *Life of Isaac Watts* complains of his poems that 'he is particularly unhappy in coining names expressive of characters', as if this were a natural expectation.

For the novel names could commonly be of two kinds, the archetypal and the realistic. In the archetypal form, of which Bunyan's *Pilgrim's Progress* (1678) provides an example that is continuously lucid, a name represents a character by resembling a word or phrase in common language, like Voltaire's Candide (innocent, open-minded), or Fielding's tutor Thwackum or his philosopher Square in *Tom Jones*. In realistic names, by contrast, a status in life is represented, as Tom Jones implies a low-born and perhaps illegitimate status, until the final revelation that the hero is rightly the heir to an estate. That the estate should be Mr Allworthy's, a figure entirely virtuous, shows how oddly these two conventions could rub shoulders in that age in the same fiction – though Allworthy is also a real West Country name. They can even be joined in deliberate incongruity: Tristram Shandy and Humphry Clinker both combine chivalric first names with comic surnames, since 'shandy' means crackbrained, and a clinker is a blunder.

The archetypal is already fading by 1800, and especially in serious fiction – at least on a conscious level. Jane Austen avoids it in her six novels, and her interest in names is entirely realistic, though realism here includes a sense of euphony as well as social status:

> In spite of Emma's resolution of never marrying, there was something in the name, in the idea of Mr Frank Churchill, which always interested her

– a delicately frivolous remark from *Emma* (ch. 14) that the heroine of Wilde's *Importance of Being Earnest* could hardly have bettered: 'It has vibrations'. But 'frank' denotes a quality, after all, and Churchill is a ducal name.

On an unconscious level, an archetypal name can succeed even in serious Victorian fiction: is the Cynthia of Elizabeth Gaskell's *Wives and Daughters* (1866) an echo of the word 'sin'? But the plausibility of the archetypal has by now narrowed, and such names for real and living persons were less common in the nineteenth century than in the eighteenth, when Capability Brown and Estimate Brown distinguished the attributes of one John Brown from another, and when a lawyer could be known as Equity Wright, father of Joseph Wright the painter.

For the Victorians an interest in names is often less naïve than this, and better informed. It can even verge on the philological. One novelist, Charlotte Mary Yonge, wrote a *History of Christian Names* in two volumes (1863), a considerable etymological treatise that includes Hebrew, Greek, Celtic and Slav. As the range widened, a sense of delicacy grew. Henry James is perhaps the most self-conscious namer among the Victorians, and his theory and practice are equally revelatory. In his notebooks he would list possibilities for future use, sometimes from newspapers. 'Fiction-mongers', he remarked to a correspondent who had objected to finding his own name in one of his stories, 'collect proper names, surnames etc – make notes and lists of any odd or unusual, as handsome or ugly ones they see or hear', whether in the press, in directories or in shop-signs.[2] One of his stories is built around the problem of nominal discordance, *Mora Montravers* (1909), where Mora and her parents dislike the name of her fiancé, Walter Puddick; though the names of some of his own heroines can clang as harsh to the ear, like Fleda Vetch in *The Spoils of Poynton* (1897). His friend Edith Wharton records that he was delighted by

> . . . the magic of ancient names, quaint or impressive, crabbed or melodious. These he would murmur over and over to himself in a low chant, finally creating characters to fit them, and sometimes whole families, with their domestic complications and matrimonial alliance, such as the Dymmes of Dymechurch, one of whom married a Sparkle, and was the mother of little Scintilla Dymme-Sparkle . . .[3]

That was in fantasising mood. In his novels he seems to have preferred a sort of transfigured realism, where names fit characters in a manner that never smacks of the crudely archetypal.

In all that, James had Thackeray for a model, and thought his names to be perfect. 'They always had a meaning', he remarked in his essay on Trollope (1883),

> and (except in his absolutely jocose productions, where they were still admirable) we can imagine, even when they are most figurative, that they should have been borne by real people. But in this, as in other respects, Trollope's hand was heavier than his master's . . .

though James admired Mrs Proudie as a perfect appellation for the domineering wife of a bishop. But he was always clear that archetypal names did not blend with realism, and thought Trollope's skittish love of them no strength to his fiction. Mr Quiverful in *Barchester Towers*, a clergyman with fourteen children, is 'too difficult to believe in', and the name is not backed by that fashion for philosophical fiction that licensed Fielding's Thwackum and Square: 'We can believe in the name and we can believe in the children, but we cannot manage the combination.' And as for Trollope's Mr Neversay Die, Mr Stickatit and, as a name for a family physician, Mr Fillgrave, 'it would be better to go back to Bunyan at once'. Trollope, who in his *Autobiography* calls such names 'feebly facetious' (ch. 6), came by the end to think so too.

A sense of onomastic fitness, for all that, is not entirely unrealistic. Some people do have names that fit them, in life; others have names that are seen, on reflection, to fit. 'For as his name is', Nabal's wife remarks to King David, in 1 Samuel 25, 'so is he; Nabal is his name, and folly is with him.' Dickens opens *Great Expectations* (1860) with a child hero who can only pronounce his own name, which is Philip, as Pip, and shows him childishly estimating the personalities of his dead parents from the shape of the letters on their tombstones. Ten years earlier, in *David Copperfield*, Dickens had already seized on a more momentous fictional possibility than that. The hero of that book is called Davy by his mother, Master Davy by Peggotty, Trot by his great-aunt, Mr Brooks of Sheffield by a cruel stepfather, and Copperfield by Mr Micawber, though Mrs Creakle solemnly addresses him as David Copperfield, in the ninth chapter, to tell him of his mother's death. The struggle to become the whole of his name, and worthy of it, is David's struggle through the length and breadth of the book. To be less than one's whole name is to be less than oneself – a mentally wounded being like Mr Dick, obsessed with King Charles's head, whose real name is Mr Richard Babley. 'But don't you call him by it, whatever you do', Miss Trotwood urges:

> He can't bear his name. That's a peculiarity of his. Though I don't know that it's much of a peculiarity, either; for he has been ill-used enough, by some that bear it, to have a mortal antipathy for it . . .' (ch. 14),

and David's own role is defined by his new name when 'Trotwood Copperfield' is indelibly marked on his new clothes in Miss Trotwood's own handwriting:

> All the other clothes which were ordered to be made for me . . . should be marked in the same way. Thus I began my new life, in a new name, and with everything new about me. (ch. 14)

At such moments Dickens seems to seize and hold – even conjoin – the polar opposites of the archetypal and the realistic, and to make of names a destiny for his hero.

ANONYMITY AND PSEUDONYMITY

This is a diminishing element over two centuries and more, and it would be an exceptional novel today that lacked the author's real name on its title-page. Since an invented name or pseudonym is a kind of anonymity, these forms need to be considered together.

In the seventeenth and eighteenth centuries, anonymity was commoner than not, especially in first editions, and especially for women, though men too could hesitate to link their names to a literary form of doubtful respectability. Mme de La Fayette's *La Princesse de Clèves* appeared anonymously in 1678, and the authoress even denied her responsibility for it in a letter, calling it *'mémoires'*, though it is not in the first person. Richardson omits his name from title-pages, and in later novels describes himself serially as an 'editor' of the preceding. To the extent that his authorship of the first novel, *Pamela*, was known, this amounts to a subtle act of self-revelation, as surely as Smollett's formula 'by the author of *Roderick Random*' or Scott's 'by the author of *Waverley*'; but the novels of all of them were technically anonymous. So were the first two editions of Fielding's *Joseph Andrews* in 1742, though the third edition of the following year was signed, as was the dedication – but not the title-page – to *Tom Jones* in 1749. *Tristram Shandy* was anonymous through all its nine volumes, and the dedication to the elder William Pitt is signed 'the author'. Marivaux and Rousseau, too, remained anonymous in their novels.

By the end of the century the convention was relaxing, though spurious 'translations' and attributions remain common. In the second half of the century, only about one-third of French novels were signed, though the movement away from anonymity remained fairly steady, decade by decade, rising to a proportion of about half and half by the 1790s. But women were slower than men to acknowledge such authorship. Mme de Villedieu (1640–83), an author of some thirty novels popular in her own century and the next, published as a professional author under her own name – unlike her contemporary Mme de La Fayette (1634–93), who was an aristocrat. Fanny Burney remained timorously unnamed as a novelist a century later, *Evelina* being composed in a disguised hand and refused by Dodsley because it was of unknown authorship; when it finally appeared in 1778, she described herself as 'frightened out of my wits from the terror of being attacked as an author', anonymous though the book was.

By the 1790s, in England as in France, signatures had grown more common. Ann Radcliffe's first successful book, *A Romance of the Forest*, appeared without her name in 1791, but was acknowledged as hers in the following year; and by 1797 two more, *Udolpho* and *The Italian*, had both appeared with her name on their title-pages. Jane Austen, however, preserved her public anonymity throughout her life, which ended in 1817, and in a manner of speaking even afterwards: *Northanger Abbey* and *Persuasion* first appeared in 1818, with no name on the title-page but the familiar formula 'by the author of *Pride and Prejudice*, *Mansfield Park* etc'. But the book was prefixed with a 'Biographical Notice of the Author' by her brother Henry, which of course revealed her name and much besides, though the notice itself was anonymous.

By the Victorian age, anonymity is largely a feminine trait in respectable fiction, and the discretion of the male falls out of fashion in the 1830s and 1840s. Scott, who died in 1832, was the last great male novelist in English to maintain it throughout his career; and William Beckford, a rich dilettante who wrote the only masterpiece of French literature ever to be composed by an Englishman, had *Vathek* (1786) published anonymously until his death in 1844. Balzac published several novels in the 1820s as a young unknown under various pseudonyms, until *Les Chouans* appeared under his name in 1829; and Henri Beyle published under the pseudonym of Stendhal in the 1830s. But Dickens soon abandoned 'Boz' for his own name, and 'by Charles Dickens' appeared unequivocally on all of them as they appeared in book form, even the first, *The Pickwick Papers*: perhaps the first great novelist of all Europe to depend so openly in all his fictions upon his own name, which was of compelling power from the age of twenty-four.

From that point on, it is anonymity that begins to look remarkable, though it is still far from rare. The three Brontë sisters, when they began to publish novels in 1847, used the pseudonyms they had chosen for their unsuccessful *Poems* of 1846, all preserving their initials: Anne became Acton Bell, Charlotte became Currer Bell, and Emily became Ellis Bell. 'We had a vague impression', wrote Charlotte in the 1850 preface to her dead sister's *Wuthering Heights*, 'that authoresses are liable to be looked on with prejudice; we had noticed how critics sometimes use for their chastisement the weapon of personality, and for their reward a flattery which is not true praise.'

That timidity survived into George Eliot, though herself a less timid woman. But in that name Mary Ann Evans invented for herself more than a pseudonym, when she began to publish fiction in 1858 – rather a character in itself, an elderly gentleman confiding in a less experienced reader; and though she gained confidence enough, in the maturer novels of the 1870s, such as *Middlemarch* (1871–2), to abandon that pretence, she kept the pseudonym and even returned to the character that had once sustained it in her last book, *Impressions of Theophrastus Such* (1879). But it is still notable that the pseudonyms of the great female novelists, such as Ellis Bell, George Sand and George Eliot, are themselves all male. Did any woman choose a female pseudonym for her fiction before 'Ouida', or Marie Louise de la Ramée (1839–1908), in the 1860s?

By the end of the century, anonymity had lost its point. The novel had achieved its own dignity as a literary kind, its composition had long since ceased to look degrading, and it was even consistent with the quality of a lady. Unsigned novels in the twentieth century are only occasional sports. They may be inspired by a sense of privacy, if highly personal, like *Olivia, by Olivia* (1949), an emotional recollection of French schooldays by Dorothy Bussy, Lytton Strachey's sister; or, as a compliment to the original, a recent attempt to complete Jane Austen's unfinished *Sanditon* in 1975, 'finished by another lady'.

MOTTOES

A motto or epigraph is a quotation, real or invented, at the head of a work – whether at the head of an entire novel, or of a chapter within it.

Eighteenth-century novels are seldom equipped with mottoes at the heads of chapters – though some, like *Tristram Shandy*, have them on the title-page, often in Latin or Greek; in *Shandy*, which appeared two volumes at a time, they link as pairs the first eight of its nine volumes, the first pair in Greek and the rest in Latin. *Tom Jones*, a decade earlier, had borne a four-word tag from Horace on its title-page; *La Nouvelle Héloïse* has a Petrarchan, and *Paul et Virginie* a Virgilian. Laclos on the title-page of his *Les Liaisons dangereuses* quotes from *La Nouvelle Héloïse* – perhaps the first use of a quotation from another novel as a motto, and a sign of advancing status.

But the vogue for mottoes is essentially nineteenth-century, the fashion very likely arising out of the periodical essay, which had often been decorated in this way: a natural parallel, though one only slowly perceived, since both forms were largely designed for unexacting instruction and entertainment, and not least for women. Addison had praised such mottoes in the *Spectator* (13 November 1711) as helpful in establishing that the essayist's notion was not eccentric or 'singular' but had classical precedent, and Boswell remarks in his *Life of Johnson* (1791) that he had heard Johnson commend them as 'the usual trappings of periodical papers.'

The beginnings are obscure. A few minor novels of the 1750s have been found with chapter-mottoes: the earliest may have been William Chaigneau's *History of Jack Connor* (1752), with mottoes from English poets and others marked 'anonimous', presumably by himself. French instances are nearly as early: Du Laurens's *Le Compère Mathieu* (1766) quotes from itself for its motto, and Gérard's *Le Comte de Valmont* (1774) from *Paradise Lost*. Jane Austen, who never uses them, refers passingly to the custom in *Emma*, where the heroine calls Mr Elton's verse-charade 'a sort of prologue to the play, a motto to the chapter', to be followed by the 'matter-of-fact prose' of a real proposal of marriage (ch. 9). But Ann Radcliffe is perhaps the first novelist of note to indulge in chapter-mottoes, in *Udolpho* (1794) and *The Italian* (1797) – mottoes no longer classical, but drawn from such native authors as Shakespeare, Milton and James Thomson.

All that suits the temper of Gothic fiction, which offers itself, however fantastically, as a view of past ages. It fits historical fiction even better. Scott gives his first novel, *Waverley* (1814), no more than a title-page motto, the apt Shakespearean tag 'Under which king, Bezonian? speak or die!'.– apt, since the hero is torn between his allegiance to George II and the Stuart cause. But his second novel, *Guy Mannering* (1815), has chapter mottoes throughout, and he keeps up the habit to the end of his days. 'It is time to think of mottoes', he writes to his publisher Ballantyne in 1814–15, implying that this was the last touch to a composition. A dozen years later, finishing *Woodstock* (1826) as a tired man, he resolved in his journal to dispense with a title-page motto, though the book already had them for chapters:

> Go to,
> D--n the mot-toe,

he resolves to himself jovially (24 March 1826). He was the first great novelist to use them so widely, but by then the notion had turned sour:

It is foolish to encourage people to expect mottoes and such like decoraments. You have no credit for success in finding them, and there is a disgrace in wanting them. It is like being in the habit of shewing feats of strength which you at length gain no praise by accomplishing, while there is some shame occurs in failure.

But they confer upon the Waverley novels an essential air of historical awareness, and the point is sharpened if one considers how incongruous they would look in Jane Austen. Historical, but hardly scholarly: Scott sometimes made them up, often quoted from memory, and could dismiss some half-forgotten source with a reference as vague as 'Old Play' or 'Anon'. But his mottoes were thought fascinating at the time, and in 1822 they were collected, with verses appearing elsewhere in his fiction, as *The Poetry Contained in the Novels, Tales and Romances of the Author of Waverley*, probably imitating the 1712 collection based on the *Tatler* and *Spectator*. In a letter of 23 March 1822, during its preparation, Scott confessed to his publisher he could hardly recall whether some of his mottoes were original or not: 'I wish you would devise some way of stating this in the title', he remarked, admitting some to have been 'botched up out of pieces and fragments of poetry floating in his memory.' The publisher, in despair, wrote an Advertisement disavowing any hope of identifying many of them, and holding 'by far the greater part' to be original.

The chapter-motto is the decorative hallmark of nineteenth-century fiction, and flourished from Scott to the First World War. Stendhal imitated Scott in this respect, among others, being the first French novelist to use chapter-mottoes in *Le Rouge et le noir* (1830), though in *La Chartreuse de Parme* (1839) he tires of them after the first two chapters. He often quotes inaccurately, sometimes inventing, sometimes attributing his own inventions to Byron or anyone he first thinks of, and showing an odd liking for Shakespeare's *Cymbeline*. He tried to romanticise the motto by turning it into an indicator of mood, whereas Scott had used it rather as a thematic summary. 'The motto (*l'épigraphe*)', he wrote in a note of May 1830, 'must increase the sensation, the emotion of the reader, if he is to have emotion, and no longer offer a more or less philosophical view of the situation.'[4] That is an ambitious view, and not universally accepted. Southey thought the whole thing such a good joke that he begins *The Doctor* (1834–47) with a 'Prelude of Mottoes', followed by a postscript, chapters numbered backwards, ante-preface and preface, with a final 'Epilude of Mottoes'. Peacock starts late, giving mottoes only to the title-pages of the first three of his seven novels; but he adds chapter-mottoes to his fourth, *Maid Marian* (1822) and keeps them up for the last three. Mrs Gaskell wrote to her publisher Chapman in April 1848 that she had 'decided on mottoes', which perhaps means that the publisher, or someone else, had suggested it; and her first novel *Mary Barton* (1848) has them – a case of the regional novel imitating the ornaments of the historical – though her later novels do not.

The great abstainers are Dickens, Thackeray and Trollope, who do not use mottoes even when writing historical novels, as if eager to supplant Scott rather than to imitate him. But George Eliot's later novels abound in diversely learned mottoes, mainly from medieval and modern languages, and in their original tongues. Sometimes she invented her own, like the remarkable little disquisition on how stories should begin at the head of *Daniel Deronda* (1876). Kipling is said to have invented all of his, though the ordinary reader is hardly expected to guess this, and a minor branch of Kipling scholarship is now dedicated to identifying them, or at least to establishing analogues.

But the fashion has barely survived in force into the present century. It now looks like an aspect of the claim of the novelist to perform the tasks of the historian or antiquary – to appear before the reader, whether seriously or ironically, as a learned sage. This is not a pose beloved of twentieth-century novelists or their readers. Today, when we want history, it is to historians that we go.

CHAPTERS

The division of novels into chapters becomes common only in the 1790s, at least in serious novels; and it is common in English before it becomes so in French.

It is not, however, unknown in earlier ages, especially in comic novels and in *contes* or tales. *Don Quixote* and its earliest versions were so divided in the seventeenth century, being a parody of romance; and the romance, like Sidney's *Arcadia*, had often been divided into long sections or 'books'. Picaresque novels were commonly divided into chapters from the start: Lesage has chapter divisions in *Gil Blas* (1715–35), and Fielding always divides his, on the stated grounds that he was writing comic epics in prose – and Homer and Virgil had divided their epics. Besides, as he explains in *Joseph Andrews* (1742), not very seriously, such divisions help the reader to skip, as inn signs encourage the traveller to pause there or 'travel on to the next' (II, 1); and butchers, after all, carve up their joints. A comic argument reflects a comic form here, or vice versa, and in the eighteenth century chapter divisions often denote the comic.

But though epic and romance both offered precedents, in the sense of being subdivided into 'books', they were not precedents that were widely accepted in early serious novels. The early memoir-novel, like *Robinson Crusoe* (1719), is often undivided, like the genuine memoir it imitates, though Prévost divides his memoir-novels into books or *livres*. Letter-novels, of course, are divided into letters rather than chapters. Mme de la Fayette's *La Princesse de Clèves*, a '*nouvelle historique*', had appeared divided into four 'parties' in 1678, but these divisions were apparently imposed by the printer, though they are oddly maintained in modern editions; and *partie* can mean a volume – a division not always made by the author's own choice.

Among early novelists, Fielding is pre-eminent in the significance he is anxious to attach to such divisions. Each book of *Joseph Andrews* and *Tom Jones* is equipped with a critical preface as its first chapter, though he tires of this device as he goes; and *Amelia* is divided into twelve books, perhaps to reflect Virgil's *Aeneid*. A contemporary reader might be reminded here of *Paradise Lost* or of Dryden's *Virgil* as easily as of the *Aeneid* itself. On the other hand, of the two French versions that appeared ten years later, in 1762, only one preserved the chapter divisions, as if these still represented an English rather than a French taste. Marivaux published his chief novels in the 1730s in instalments, each a *partie*, and without chapters; and Rousseau insisted that his epistolary *La Nouvelle Héloïse* should be set up in six 'parties', each a structural unit.

Classical forerunners could help to explain the growing fashion for chapter divisions and chapter headings in the eighteenth century. Milton had equipped his epic with summaries or 'arguments', after all, and Pope's *Iliad* (1715) is set out in similar fashion. Fielding's grasp of all this is essentially cervantic, and he is fond of chapter headings like 'Which Some Readers Will Think Too Short, and Others Too Long' (*Joseph Andrews* III, 8), a facetiously uninformative mode that Dickens and Thackeray revived. Smollett expands Fielding's chapter titles into fuller arguments, in *Roderick Random* (1748), so that it would be possible to follow the whole course of that novel by reading in outline the table of contents.

But such fullness is exceptional. The 'argument', in the epic or

Miltonic sense, suits neither the memoir-novel nor the epistolary, and by the nineteenth century it has little more than the force of parody, though by then a parody of Fielding and Smollett rather than of the epic itself. Most novelists since Jane Austen have been content to number their chapters, as she does, and leave it at that. But in Jane Austen and elsewhere the enumeration, presumably imposed by the printer, can recommence with each volume.

The chapter division appears to have been an English fashion, at least for serious novels, and was borrowed by the French, or accepted by them only slowly. It is exceptional in serious eighteenth-century French novels, at least before the 1790s. But Constant's *Adolphe* (1816), short as it is, is so divided, and Stendhal in the 1830s uses it thoroughly. When Balzac sent the manuscript of *Le Père Goriot* (1834–5) to his printers, he had divided it into chapters in the English manner, but the printer removed these divisions, presumably to save paper, and printed it without a break, though modern editions have restored his divisions. By now all that is taken for granted, and Fielding may have been powerfully responsible for this acceptance. Indeed his sister Sarah, in her *History of Charlotte Summers* (1749), if indeed it is hers, acclaims him loyally as 'very full in displaying the convenience of these kinds of divisions', and goes on:

> I look upon these sort of divisions . . . to be like the acts and scenes in a play; the main design of which must be to give time for shifting the scenes and conveying the audience without hurry or apparent absurdity to and from the several places and apartments where the poet had laid his action (ch. 2),

applauding her brother's wit in entitling his chapters. The analogy with theatre is engaging, even revealing; and in an age that read aloud as well as silently, there may have been practical considerations in favour of interrupting narrative in an intelligible way. Proust once remarked that he admired nothing in Flaubert more than a certain gap between passages in *L'Éducation sentimentale*, and in his own novel he prefers gaps to chapter divisions. Though the chapter, by now, looks so natural to the novel as to be taken for granted, its lineage is revealing. If it is indeed descended from ancient epic by way of its later editors, translators and imitators, then it represents one of the few evidences of that heroic literature to survive into the present age.

GLOSSARIES AND INDEXES

Of all kinds of books, novels need indexes least – or so one is disposed, unreflectively, to say. But they occasionally have them.

This may seem less surprising if one recalls their function as edifying treatises or tracts. Richardson's *Clarissa*, for example, was equipped with an appendix of 'moral and instructive sentiments'; and his *Grandison* concludes with a substantial 'Index Historical and Characteristicall' to the whole novel, over a hundred pages long, where 'characteristicall' refers to moral characteristics and adages as well as to characters; together with a four-page alphabetical register of similes and allusions. This was what some readers wanted. Samuel Johnson had already written to Richardson about *Clarissa* begging for an *index rerum*, since it was 'not a performance to be read with eagerness, and laid aside for ever; but will be occasionally consulted by the busy, the aged, and the studious' (9 March 1751). And novels could be encyclopædic as well as moral, like *Le Voyage du jeune Anarchasis* of Jean-Jacques Barthélemy, a scholarly Frenchman, which appeared in 1788 after thirty years of research, describing a young Scythian touring Greece in the time of Alexander the Great. Each volume ends with historical notes; and the whole massive work, which was designed to educate effortlessly in the details of Greek antiquity, ends with convenient tables and indexes.

Novels can occasionally need glossaries, too, such as an edition of Rabelais in 1751, *Le Rabelais moderne*, where sixteenth-century terms had to be explained to eighteenth-century Frenchmen. Rousseau had used footnotes to explain Swiss terms in *La Nouvelle Héloïse*; and Maria Edgeworth's *Castle Rackrent* was fitted out at the last moment in 1800 with a 'Glossary' of Irish words and phrases which is really a commentary, being arranged page by page rather than alphabetically, and composed by the novelist herself when the book was already in proof; it was awkwardly printed before the novel in the first edition, to suit the printer's convenience, and moved to its proper place at the end only with the second edition. Since *Rackrent* already had explanatory footnotes, it emerged under an excess of apparatus; but then the first regional novel in the language naturally bears about itself an apologetic air. Such prefatory material, in any case, is not unique: in 1747, Mme de Grafigny's *Lettres d'une Péruvienne* had included an introduction offering details concerning the history, customs and even language of Peru, by someone who had never been there.

Fortunately, perhaps, the notion of editorial apparatus never took root, and the ordinary assumption surrounding novels was and remains that they should explain themselves. Jane Austen never used notes or glossaries, or felt the need for them. Scott did, especially historical notes, sometimes added in later editions to defend himself against the complaints of reviewers. So did his English disciple Harrison Ainsworth: the index to his *Tower of London* (1840), for example, functions doubly as an index and a series of historical explanations of persons and places in Tudor England. That must have made it look helpful to young persons, but at the same time artistically naïve. Dickens's two historical novels – *Barnaby Rudge* (1841) and *A Tale of Two Cities* (1859) – have no apparatus, and George Eliot's *Romola* (1863) only allows itself a few footnotes and a single end-note explaining that Savonarola's sermon is not a translation but 'a free representation' of the way he preached. A scrupulous afterthought: but even novels educative in their historical purpose were felt, by then, to survive better without the crutch of an explanatory aid.

NOTES

1. Gilbert Ryle, 'Jane Austen and the Moralists', *Oxford Review* 1 (1966).
2. Bertram Brewster, 'The Capadose Family', in Isaac Da Costa, *Noble Families among the Sephardic Jews* (Oxford: 1936) p. 187 note, from a letter of 13 October 1896.
3. Edith Wharton, *A Backward Glance* (New York: 1934) p. 249.
4. Stendhal, *Melanges intimes et marginalia* (Paris: 1936) II, 78.

6 *Beginning and Ending*

Anyone who tells a story must solve the problem of sealing off his narrative at both ends.

In anecdotes, as they are commonly told, the solution is often ready-made. In advanced social fiction this is rarely so. 'The whole of everything', Henry James remarks in his *Notebooks*, 'is never told; you can only take what groups together' (p. 18). But such groupings can easily look amorphous, and there is a sense in which the novelist is forced to make a start where there is no true start, or an end where there is no true end. *Tristram Shandy* mercilessly parodies this dilemma, with Sterne posing as the zealous narrator who cannot tell you what happened without telling you what happened before that, and before that . . .

'Really, universally, relations stop nowhere', James remarks in his preface to *Roderick Hudson*. That is the absolute view. In practice the classic English novel often begins with a birth, like *Crusoe*, and ends with a marriage, like *Tom Jones*. But before birth there is gestation, as Shandy knew, and before gestation a conception, and before conception a secret message passed between those who are about to become parents. And marriage, though it ends one system of relations, starts another.

One might reply to James that the problem is in some degree self-induced, and that a novelist can choose to worry about it or not. The climax of that sort of anxiety lies in the period between the death of Dickens in 1870 and that of James in 1916. Sterne and his readers saw it less as a problem than as a chance to play games with the conventions of narrative. There is little Jamesian anxiety in eighteenth-century fiction because there is little of the sense of fictional dignity that gives rise to that sort of anxiety. In the comic novel, especially, the conventions of fiction are fair game, to be mocked and defied; they can even amount to licences in themselves. The author of a letter-novel, Fielding remarks, 'is freed from the regular beginnings and conclusions of stories, with some other formalities' (preface to Sarah Fielding, *Familiar Letters*, 1747).

But as dignity grows, so does unease. The triumph of omniscience after 1800 confers power on the novelist, and something like that sense of responsibility that power is supposed to bring. Confidence can look godlike, for the mid-Victorians, and David Masson in his *British Novelists and Their Styles* (1859) is content, like Flaubert, to employ the divine analogy:

> The novelist, as the creator of his mimic world, is also its providence; he makes the laws that govern it; he conducts the lines of events to their issue; he winds up all according to his judicial wisdom. (p. 23)

Nothing anxious in this view, and Dickens, Thackeray and Trollope all behave as if it were so: in *Vanity Fair*, eleven years earlier, Thackeray had offered his reader a walk through the Fair 'to examine the shops and shows there' (ch. 19), ending with the cry 'Vanity of vanities' and the dismissive sentence: 'Come, children, let us shut up the box and the puppets, for our play is played out.'

★

But are the characters of the great mid-Victorian novels merely puppets? and is a puppet play something to be begun and ended at will? Masson and Thackeray are hardly offering a licence to the novelist to begin and end as he pleases: they plainly see stories as convention-bound. *Vanity Fair* begins with the girlhood of two heroines of contrasting temperament, and ends with the happiness of the deserving Amelia and the unmasking of Becky. The reader is cajoled with talk of vanities and sweetmeats, but there is an iron logic in the plots of such books as *Vanity Fair* and *Barchester Towers* which, if not invariable, is at least highly conformable to the expectations of the age, and utterly lucid. 'The good end happily, the bad unhappily', as a character remarks in Oscar Wilde. 'That is what fiction means.' And one way to study the logic of such stories is to consider how they begin and end.

BEGINNINGS

In that confident phase of European fiction, or the century and a half and more between *Crusoe* (1719) and 1880, when Flaubert and George

Eliot died, there were broadly three ways in which a novelist might begin his narrative.

1. By determination of place and time. This represents a major technical shift for long fictions, since the classic opening for epic and seventeenth-century romance had been *in medias res*, and it may be hard now to recapture that sense of shock that the classic opening of the memoir-novel may once have been designed to inflict: 'I was born in that place, and in the year . . .'. This opening is so fully naturalised into the novel in the course of the eighteenth century that it continues long after the memoir has lost its vogue, and often in terms less blunt than these. Balzac can begin with a date; and *Vanity Fair* opens in a manner only faintly removed from that:

> While the present century was in its teens . . . there drove up to . . . Chiswick Mall. . . .

That puts the place and time as London in the 1810s, which many readers in 1847–8 could conveniently recall, and which many more had heard tell of. Since the two heroines are shortly to be introduced as school-leavers, it establishes a comfortable presumption that the time scheme will be drawn up gently in the course of the book towards the present, as in many an eighteenth-century memoir-novel. (In the fourth chapter Thackeray uses the phrase 'forty years ago', though that must be approximate, as the novel includes the Battle of Waterloo.) In an earlier novel, Harrison Ainsworth's *Old St Paul's* (1841), which tells of the Great Plague and Fire of London in 1665–6, each of the five books is dated by month and year – an over-explicit device that Thackeray may have been eager to avoid. Dickens's famous opening to *Bleak House* (1853) is still further removed from the explicit. It begins in note form – a surrealist syntax for a surreal world which suddenly expands outwards at a dizzying pace:

> London. Michaelmas Term lately over, and the Lord Chancellor sitting in Lincoln's Inn Hall. Implacable November weather. As much mud in the streets as if the waters had but newly retired from the face of the earth, and it would not be wonderful to meet a Megalosaurus, forty feet long or so, waddling like an elephantine lizard up Holborn Hill.

All that is highly efficient, though parodied as fantasy: the place is London, then, and the time is now, and winter.

Jane Austen begins all her six novels except *Pride and Prejudice* in the determining way, though she is usually less specific with dates than a Victorian novelist would be, as if confident that her readers will understand the silent device 'In England, now' to stand above all her fictions. *Sense and Sensibility* (1811), the first to appear, begins with some brisk information about the standing of the family: 'The family of Dashwood had long been settled in Sussex. Their estate was large. . . .' *Mansfield Park* (1814), the third, uses 'ago', a word that can only apply to a past period seen from the present: 'About thirty years ago, Miss Maria Ward of Huntingdon, with only seven thousand pounds, had the good luck to captivate Sir Thomas Bertram. . . .' *Emma* (1816) and *Northanger Abbey* (1818) begin in a slightly more allusive manner, describing the heroine in terms at once ironic and yet highly predictive of plot. 'Handsome, clever and rich', Emma is called, having 'lived nearly twenty-one years in the world with very little to distress or vex her', to invite a harshly admonitory reflection from the reader. 'No one who had ever seen Catherine Morland in her infancy', so *Northanger Abbey* begins, 'would have supposed her born to be a heroine' – an absurdity confirmed by the determining details of her parentage, all amiably ridiculous:

> Her father was a clergyman, without being neglected or poor, and a very respectable man, though his name was Richard – and he had never been handsome. He had a considerable independence, besides two good livings – and he was not in the least addicted to locking up his daughters.

The last to appear, *Persuasion* (1818), begins in exceptionally explicit terms, though enlivened by the device of the heroine's father reading his favourite page in the Baronetage, which is the page that contains his own entry: 'Walter Elliot, born March 1, 1760, married, July 15, 1784, Elizabeth. . . .'

2. By plunging into the story *in medias res*, or without determination of place or time – such details being delayed for a paragraph, or a page, or even longer. This harks back to the epic; but it is effectively different to the extent that epics commonly tell a story already known to the reader. In novels it will work best where an assumption can easily be made about a period or theme the author is known to prefer. Most readers know that Jane Austen and Henry James never wrote historical novels, and that Scott wrote no other kind: the guesswork is rarely taxing, and it is hardly tolerable that it should be.

Type 2 is less than usual in eighteenth-century fiction, but a growing preference since. The dialogue opening is an instance of it, but that is a device rare before the Victorians. It may even be doubted if indeterminacy is commonplace in Victorian fiction. Flaubert begins *Madame Bovary* (1857) in that way: 'Nous étions a l'étude . . .'; and Dickens occasionally attempts it, most strikingly in his last novel, *Edwin Drood* (1870), which starts puzzlingly in the scattered consciousness of an opium victim. But it is foreign to the genius of Trollope, who held determinacy to be an unswerving principle. As he argues at the start of *Is He Popenjoy?* (1878),

> I would that it were possible so to tell a story that a reader should beforehand know every detail of it up to a certain point, or be so circumstanced that he might be supposed to know,

as happens when we tell one another stories about people we know in life. He was against indeterminacy, or 'jumping at once into the middle', on the grounds that the novelist has 'to hark back, and to begin again from the beginning – not always very comfortably after the abnormal brightness of his few opening pages'. That is a serious aesthetic point: that a novel has no business to deceive the reader into thinking it livelier than it is. Ford Madox Ford, in his memoir *Joseph Conrad* (1924), tells how he and his friend disagreed on the point, Conrad preferring a leap into story and a harking back, or 'the dramatic opening', Ford 'the more pensive approach'. It was always a friendly difference between them:

> The disadvantage of the dramatic opening is that after the dramatic passage is done you have to go back to getting your characters in, a proceeding that the reader is apt to dislike. The danger with the reflective opening is that the reader is apt to miss being gripped at once by the story. Openings are therefore of necessity always affairs of compromise (p. 173).

On the other hand, an indeterminate opening can tantalise and seduce. Consider George Eliot's opening to *Daniel Deronda* (1876):

> Was she beautiful or not beautiful? and what was the secret of form or expression which gave the dynamic quality to her glance? . . .

These questions are not those of a narrator, though the reader might at first be forgiven for supposing it: they are in the mind of Deronda himself as he watches an unknown Englishwoman in a continental casino. But it is only here, in her last novel, that George Eliot allowed herself to play this innocent trick on her readers.

The same evolution is visible in Henry James. His earlier novels usually start determinately, but he moves rapidly towards the *Deronda* style of opening. *The Awkward Age* (1899) begins: 'Save when it happened to rain, Vanderbank always walked home . . .'; *The Wings of the Dove* (1902): 'She waited, Kate Croy, for her father to come in . . .'; and *The Golden Bowl* (1904): 'The Prince had always liked his London, when it had come to him . . .' – a compelling little nuance, since one expects rather 'when he had come to it'.

In the twentieth century the indeterminate is probably the commonest of styles; so much so that a reader might now be almost surprised to be told the essential facts in a first sentence, or even in the first paragraph. 'My first impression', Christopher Isherwood's *Mr Norris Changes Trains* (1935) begins, 'was that the stranger's eyes were of an unusually light blue', and it is not until the second page that one discovers that the scene concerns two Englishmen, and on a train abroad.

3. A thematic opening, or aphorism.

Some are unforgettable:

I was ever of opinion, that the honest man who married and brought up a large family, did more service than he who continued single, and only talked of population. (Goldsmith, *The Vicar of Wakefield* [1766])

It is a truth universally acknowledged, that a single man in possession of a good fortune must be in want of a wife. (Jane Austen, *Pride and Prejudice* [1813])

All happy families resemble one another, but each unhappy family is unhappy in its own way. (Tolstoy, *Anna Karenina* [1875–7])

Under certain circumstances there are few hours in life more agreeable than the hour dedicated to the ceremony known as afternoon tea. (Henry James, *The Portrait of a Lady* [1881])

Thematic openings were already common in seventeenth-century fiction, and were usually meant to be literally understood. But the instances quoted are not quite like that. They look secretively ironic as well as helpfully directive, as if announcing a theme of the novel and urging the alert reader not to believe it at the same time. Perhaps this is an aspect of advancing realism: there is something faintly parodic about beginning a story of our own times with a general observation, if only because modern societies are less hospitable to the proverb and the commonplace than the Europe for which epics and romances were written. The modern novel belongs to a more sceptical time. Since Fielding begins all his three novels with general observations, it may be revealing to consider them together.

It is a trite but true observation that examples work more forcibly on the mind than precepts. (*Joseph Andrews* [1742])

An author ought to consider himself, not as a gentleman who gives a private or eleemosynary treat, but rather as one who keeps a public ordinary, at which all persons are welcome for their money. (*Tom Jones* [1749])

The various accidents which befell a very worthy couple after their uniting in the state of matrimony will be the subject of the following history. (*Amelia* [1751])

Only the third is entirely unplayful: the first wryly announces itself as trite, and the second beguilingly implies that Fielding (exceptionally, for an eighteenth-century English novelist) was himself a gentleman. The thematic opening is often ambiguous in its standing, and alerts the reader to a sort of provisional scepticism. Fielding's notion of the trite is echoed by Jane Austen in her one attempt at the form, in *Pride and Prejudice*, in her mocking phrase about 'a truth universally acknowledged'; and James plays a similar game when he uses the portentous words 'dedicated' and 'ceremony' of so simple a matter as afternoon tea.

And yet it would be hard to argue that these novelists are radically misleading their readers. *Joseph Andrews* undeniably offers moral lessons through examples, and *Pride and Prejudice* ends with an eligible bachelor marrying the heroine. If irony is at work at all here, it can only be a double irony: a view offered in seemingly bad faith is eventually revealed as true. All that is doubtless designed to antici-

pate objection. It is the harder to complain of the trite, when the trite
so openly proclaims itself to be that.

ENDINGS

Two novels, Sterne's *Sentimental Journey* (1768) and Samuel Beckett's
Malone meurt (1951), end whimsically without even a mark of punctuation. But an ending, to be most fully and convincingly that, needs
more than a period. It needs to be required by the novel as a totality.
Stories have their own logic, though hardly an invariable one. In his
autobiography *Something of Myself* (1937), Kipling tells how one day
he mentioned to his father that *Kim* was finished. 'Did *it* stop, or you?'
his father asked; and when Kipling replied 'It', his father remarked:
'Then it oughtn't to be too bad' (p. 140).

The logic of stories, however variable, makes for a higher degree of
uniformity in endings than beginnings can be said to possess. John
Fowles's *The French Lieutenant's Woman* (1969) offers alternative endings to the reader, but each is classic in form, and the English novel
between Fielding and Dickens notoriously ends with a marriage, at its
most characteristic, and a promise of happiness to come. All of Jane
Austen's six novels conclude in this familiar way, though the last
sentence of all can produce a witty variant. Whereas *Emma* stops with
a phrase about 'the perfect happiness of the union' of Emma and Mr
Knightley, *Persuasion* concludes with a surprising shaft of wit:

> She gloried in being a sailor's wife, but she must pay the tax of quick
> alarm for belonging to that profession which is, if possible, more
> distinguished in its domestic virtues than in its national impor-
> tance.

It is startling that Jane Austen should end her last novel with a burst
of praise for the profession of her own family, and the insertion of 'if
possible' is impressively deft. Her nephew, in his *Memoir* (1870), tells
that this was not the original ending, which failed to satisfy her as
being 'tame and flat'; and how she awoke one morning to cancel a
chapter and write two others, 'entirely different, in its stead' (ch. 11).
Effects as chiselled as these, it is clear, were won at the cost of great
pains.

In the classic phase of English fiction – but not, seemingly, in the
Russian, French or American – it was widely accepted that a novel
should end in serenity. Trollope occasionally mocks the unrealism of
that convention, but he observes it too. 'The end of a novel, like the

end of a children's dinner-party, must be made up of sweetmeats and sugar-plums', he remarks in the last chapter of *Barchester Towers* (1857). Three years later, Dickens was to soften the ending of *Great Expectations*, at Bulwer Lytton's suggestion. But here the very logic of his story favours the Trollopian view, and his first version now looks at once feebly and inaptly revengeful. In the first draft Pip meets Estella in Piccadilly after two years of separation; her cruel husband has died, and she has married a country doctor; and her manner suggests that 'suffering had been stronger than Miss Havisham's teaching, and had given her a heart to understand what my heart used to be'. It is hard to see why anyone should prefer this to the revised version, which represents one of the most realised of all the happy endings of fiction:

> I took her hand in mine, and we went out of the ruined place; and as the morning mists had risen long ago when I first left the forge, so the evening mists were rising now, and in all the broad expanse of tranquil light they showed to me, I saw no shadow of another parting from her.

That magisterial period gathers up a scattering of hints, after all, notably in its mention of mists and shadows. When Pip left for London in the nineteenth chapter, the rising mist had symbolised his hopes of success in the capital:

> We changed again, and yet again, and it was too late and too far to go back, and I went on. And the mists had all solemnly risen now, and the world lay spread before me,

Dickens adding here in headline capitals: 'THIS IS THE END OF THE FIRST STAGE OF PIP'S EXPECTATIONS'. And the shadow at the end of the novel recalls another haunting detail: the degraded faces of Estella's unguessed parents that tell of an origin even humbler than his own: 'What *was* the nameless shadow which again in that one instant had passed?' (ch. 32). The perfection of a last sentence, composed on deeper reflection, gathers up the threads of story into a single and masterful grasp.

★

For a century and more, fiction moves towards that sense of decision, and above all towards endings that are linked to beginnings in a relation that is more than rhetorical. To the modern eye, early eighteenth-century novels can look unacceptably perfunctory in their conclusions, as if allowing for the possibility of a sequel, whether by the novelist himself or by someone else. As late as 1784, Mme de Charrière ended her little letter-novel *Lettres-neuchâteloises* with an 'editorial' note: 'The publisher of these *Letters* does not know whether they have a sequel or, if they do, whether he could obtain it' – presumably waiting to judge demand by the verdict of sales. The early memoir-novel often ends indecisively, its hero alive and active enough to be capable of writing an account of his own life. Sometimes, like Marivaux's *La Vie de Marianne* (1731–41), which is unfinished, the plot wanders off so inconclusively that it is difficult to see how it could ever have been terminated. Defoe's *Roxana* (1724) ends, if ending it be, with no more than a laconic remark by the heroine that, after a period of good fortune, 'I was brought so low again, that my repentance seemed to be only the consequence of my misery, as of my crime'; but no details of that misery follow, perhaps because Defoe had vague thoughts of a continuation. Four years earlier, *Moll Flanders* had ended with nothing more than a resolution by Moll and her husband 'to spend the remainder of our years in sincere penitence for the wicked lives we have lived' – an ending that could have been offered earlier or later, at will.

The modern reader is inclined to ask for something more than this, and it is only as paradox that he can willingly entertain the notion of a story that could go on indefinitely, or stop at any moment. In *Les Faux-monnayeurs* (1925) André Gide remarks teasingly that every end should be itself a starting-point, and that he would have liked to finish his novel with the words 'Might be continued' (III, 13). Michael Frayn's first novel, *The Tin Man* (1965), does end much like that, with a computer beginning to compose the novel one has just read; but that is less like an indeterminate ending than a serpent with its tail in its mouth. No twentieth-century novel one can easily think of ends as indeterminately as *Roxana*. We commonly demand of our fictions now that time must have a stop.

The most decisive endings to stories, by long tradition, are a wedding and a death. The memoir-novel can accommodate the first, but hardly the second – unless, that is, it steps out of its own frame and admits a postscript by an 'editor' describing the death of its hero. The letter-novel can readily do either: Richardson's *Pamela* (1740) ends with the hero winning the hand of Mr B. in virtuous marriage, and

Clarissa (1748) with the heroine's death – a high catastrophe terminating a tragedy of manners – with a 'Conclusion' by Belford nearly 10,000 words long, describing the fates of her survivors in the story, including two weddings, and finally a postscript on justice and the idea of tragedy. Rousseau's *La Nouvelle Héloïse* (1761) ends with the death of Julie in an odour of sanctity; Laclos's *Les Liaisons dangereuses* (1782) with two deaths, a disgrace and a claustration.

By the 1740s more novelists than one felt a duty to satisfy the curiosity of their readers concerning the end of most, or all, of their characters. Defoe does not bother with it, but Lesage, Richardson and Fielding often do: *Tom Jones* (1749) ends with a series of paragraphs, each devoted to a character or two, before a final reminder of the felicity of Mr Jones and his Sophia. *Amelia* (1752), in its last chapter, assures the reader that 'Amelia is still the finest woman in England of her age'. This is common in English novels down to the death of Trollope in 1882. Jane Austen always does it, though unlike Fielding she maintains the past tense to the very end. Fielding, like Lesage in *Gil Blas* in 1735, prefers to draw his stories up into the present: 'Sophia hath already produced him two fine children, a boy and a girl . . .' – a device much loved of Dickens and Trollope, and one that makes for the cosiest of endings. We leave Mr Pickwick still alive at the end of *The Pickwick Papers*, and alive now:

> Mr Pickwick is somewhat infirm now; but he retains all his former juvenility of spirit, and may still be frequently seen contemplating the pictures in the Dulwich Gallery. . . . The children idolize him,

while in Trollope the convention is luxuriously indulged, an entire chapter often being given over to a recital of the fate of the characters, one by one and in the present tense. Mr Harding 'is still Precentor of Barchester', he assures his readers at the end of *Barchester Towers*, with much of the same sort, and he even seems to have nurtured the whimsical notion of some of his characters that they survived his books for years. 'I do not doubt but that they are living happily together to this day', he remarks happily in his *Autobiography* (1883), (ch. 6) of the heroine of *The Three Clerks* (1858), after an interval of a quarter century. Such touches were well calculated to annoy the young Henry James. But they may have helped to diminish the sum total of letters from strangers that Trollope felt obliged to answer, or importunate questions put to him in clubs and country houses –

sealing off his fictions with a battery of information that leaves no room for questioning.

Even before Trollope was dead, however, the convention was felt to be over-cosy and over-traditional among ambitious talents. Flaubert ends *Madame Bovary* (1857) in the present tense, but by no means cosily. George Eliot uses it only sparingly, and with evident scepticism; *Felix Holt* (1866) ends with a tart remark in the present tense, but it substantially declines to play the old game:

> As to the town in which Felix Holt now resides, I will keep that a secret, lest he should be troubled by any visitor having the insufferable motive of curiosity. . . . There is a young Felix, who has a great deal more science than his father, but not much more money.

Her more memorable conclusions are sonorous rather than informative, where she points a moral in calm, unhurried terms. *Middlemarch* (1872) ends in high admonitory vein:

> But the effect of her being on those around her was incalculably diffusive: for the growing good of the world is partly dependent on unhistoric acts; and that things are not so ill with you and me as they might have been, is half owing to the number who lived faithfully a hidden life, and rest in unvisited tombs.

Henry James extends that expatiatory style of ending backwards through the novel, so that the characters progressively see and expound truths to the reader: not a single truth, at his most characteristic, but a complex one seen in all its complexity. It is even a question whether a James novel *can* be finished. 'We shall never be again as we were!' Kate Croy exclaims at the end of *The Wings of the Dove* (1902), contemplating with her lover the self-sacrifice the dead heroine has been capable of performing for them both. In an outward sense the events may be perfunctory, and in James they are often better so, since he does not excel at describing action. But hands are raised in admiration at an example recently set and still more recently apprehended in its full significance. His taste is for an act more symbolic than visible, and it is never like the simple symbolism of Richardson's Clarissa, who dies smiling with the sacred name on her lips. Chekov, who was born some twenty years after James, remarked in a letter that his instinct told him to end a novel by 'artfully concentrating for the reader an impression of the entire work' (9 April 1888). That is a very late Victorian demand: George Eliot and Hardy and James would have echoed it, but not Dickens, Thackeray or Trollope.

To the modern mind, this is the final kind of finality, and by far the most satisfying: a speech or thought that casts its light backwards and forwards – back into the novel it concludes, and forward into an unspoken future. 'Why can't we be friends now?', an Englishman asks an Indian at the end of Forster's *Passage to India* (1924), while the earth replies 'No, not yet', and the heavens, 'No, not there'. The device is very modern. It rejects a classic event like a marriage or a death in favour of a declaration that epitomises the total meaning of a work. Of course, it is a novelist's ending rather than a novel's, and Kipling's father might not have approved. It is Forster who ends *A Passage to India*, so the elder Kipling might well have objected: 'it' does not. For the moment, at least, in the long unended struggle between form and story, form has won.

7 *Tense and Time*

Of all the senses, Samuel Johnson once remarked, time is 'the most obsequious to the imagination'.

A novelist might reasonably think himself its master, then, and not its slave. Though he may not be free to do anything he pleases with his time scheme, it is certain that he is in no way bound to do only one thing: to let the action move steadily forward. Freedom from that bond existed before the novel was born, in epic and romance; and in the novel itself it was announced at least as early as Fielding, and exploited at least as early as Sterne.

It is odd, then, that modern critics should sometimes speak of chronology in fiction as traditional: given that many early novels, like epics before them, start *in medias res* and zigzag as intricately as Proust, the assumption suggests an ignorance of what the tradition of fiction is. Odd, too, that any novelist should ever have seen the novel as bounded by time in its most constraining or ever-advancing sense. And yet that constraint has been felt more strongly in this century, if anything, than in its predecessors. Sterne's experiment in telling a story backwards has not ceased to look strange after two centuries: if anything, it looks stranger than ever. Novelists since the First World War have only occasionally made a dash for that sort of liberty. 'There is always a clock' in a novel, E. M. Forster complained in his *Aspects of the Novel* (1927), and it always moves forward, as good clocks do, however much the novelist may wish otherwise. Forster's claim here is hard to swallow as historical:

> The author may dislike his clock. Emily Brontë in *Wuthering Heights* tried to hide hers. Sterne, in *Tristram Shandy*, turned his upside down. Marcel Proust, still more ingenious, kept altering the hands .... All these devices are legitimate, but none of them contravene

83

our thesis: the basis of a novel is a story, and a story is a narrative of events arranged in a time sequence (ch. 2).

It is hard to imagine what contravention would look like if these three instances do not contravene. Emily Brontë invented the most elaborate scheme for her only novel, with one first-person narrative built inside another; and so elaborate is the dating, marked at the start as '1801', that editors have succeeded in fixing years for the birth, marriage and death of the principal characters: Catherine Earnshaw, born summer 1765, died 20 March 1784, and the like; the chief events of the novel occurring sixty years and more before it appeared in 1847, though the story runs down to 1801, ending where it began.

All that is very nineteenth-century; eighteenth-century novelists can be carelessly inconsistent about details, and can defy probability to the point of the preposterous: Mme de Grafigny's *Lettres péruviennes* (1746), for instance, begins with the Spanish conquest of Peru in the early sixteenth century, and ends in eighteenth-century Paris, with the same characters. But *Wuthering Heights* puts no such strain on credulity, and it does not hide its clock. It might rather be said to brandish it. And 'arranged in a time-sequence' is just what *Tristram Shandy* is not: its events are outrageously disarranged.

But the novel since then has allowed itself to grow time-bound. Its liberty has not advanced over two centuries and more, and licences which the eighteenth century would have taken for granted, or at least taken easily, have been accepted only grudgingly in this century, or regarded as matter for excited critical comment. Many of the time devices of the French *nouveau roman* would have seemed rather ordinary to a contemporary of Samuel Johnson, who might equally have found Henry James's agony over the question hard to understand. 'The eternal time-question', as James calls it in the 1907 preface to *Roderick Hudson* –

> always there and always formidable; always insisting on the *effect* of the great lapse and passage, or the 'dark backward and abysm', by the terms of truth; and on the effect of compression, of composition and form, by the terms of literary arrangement. It is really a business to terrify all but the stoutest hearts into abject omission and mutilation. . . .

But James's mountain was a molehill to Fielding, who saw himself in

Tom Jones as 'the founder of a new province of writing', and for just that reason its dictator. The novel, he announced there, was under no obligation to move forward relentlessly like a stage-coach, 'which performs constantly the same course, empty as well as full'. Like the epic out of which it allegedly grew, and like the writings of historians, it makes intelligent distinctions.

> It is our purpose, in the ensuing pages, to pursue a contrary method. When any extraordinary scene presents itself, . . . we shall spare no pains nor paper to open it at large to our readers; but if whole years should pass without producing anything worthy his notice, we shall not be afraid of a chasm in our history, but shall hasten on to matters of consequence, and leave out periods of time totally unobserved. . . . (II, 1)

That brisk good sense is critically more emancipated than James or Forster, and its mention of 'history' seizes on a point of some potency: that since history is not evenly chronological, the cause of ver- isimilitude does not require the novelist to be that either. The time it takes to read is nothing like the time that elapses in narrative, whether true or fictional. What historian ever felt bound to recite his events always and invariably at the pace in which they occurred, or even in that order? It is certain that Tacitus and Clarendon did not behave in that way, or Gibbon and Macaulay either.

The history of the novel, then, is in some ways one of lost liberty, though not of a liberty steadily or totally lost. The European novel since Scott has stepped out of chronology less often, it seems likely, than its predecessors did. It has not recently allowed itself the exemplary tale beloved of Cervantes or Fielding, for example, spoken by a character at length and outside the principal time scheme. It has not jostled the reader's sense of time as disturbingly as the great letter-novels involving several correspondents, such as *Clarissa* or *Les Liaisons dangereuses*, which require a concentration of a kind the ordinary Victorian or twentieth-century reader seems unready to bring to fiction. And it has only occasionally, and then startlingly, put time into reverse, forward, and reverse again, as Sterne once ventured to do. In this respect *Shandy* is a more radical experiment than anything by Proust or William Faulkner.

By the early decades of the nineteenth century, the novel had achieved a settled dignity and a range of shared expectations between author and reader that is more earnest than playful, and which is certainly impatient of play for its own sake. Dickens's indifference to that sort of game, like Thackeray's, Trollope's or George Eliot's, is remarkable, outside *Bleak House.* But that indifference is an aspect of the security, the sheer cosiness, of the great Victorian novel, which is most commonly set in a familiar world where formal experiment would disturb something rightly precious to author and reader alike. Such classics survive by a sense of internal consistency, of which Thackeray's *Henry Esmond* is perhaps the most complete aspiration, and that sense would be jolted and even shattered by an element of disordered time. This is a precious thing, even if it has dampened the experimental ardour of fiction. 'Why is the past so beautiful?' Carlyle asked in his journal in 1835, and he returns an answer that is still satisfying: 'The element of *fear* is withdrawn from it, for one thing. That is all safe, while the present and future are all so dangerous.'

★

I propose now to consider certain techniques of time in fiction.

TENSE

Why are most novels mainly composed in the past tense? And why is it that when readers or critics recount the plot of a novel, or any part of one, they commonly translate it into the present?

The simplest answer to these questions is that we conventionally associate past tense with telling a story, and present tense with analysis. In ordinary conversation, it is worth noting, anecdotes are usually in the past tense, even when they are offered as fictitious: 'An Englishman, a Scotsman and an Irishman *were* walking down a street. . . .'

The terms 'present' and 'past', then, are at least partially misnomers: these tenses symbolise something other than points on a time scale. But they are not total misnomers. We continue to offer a provisional welcome to the historical claim, even in the wildest fictions. The story-teller can even announce 'This is true' before his anecdote, usually without much hope of persuasion, or begin 'A funny thing happened as I was coming here today . . .'; and the convention, however implausible, is reassuring. The twentieth century has not abandoned the whole, or even the greater part, of Richardson's entreaty to pretend momentarily that known fictions are true. We still suspend disbelief, and willingly.

No novel, to my knowledge, has ever been written in the future tense, though science fiction is about a future time. We may divide the main tenses of novels, then, into three broad classes: past, present and mixed.

1. *Past.* This signals that a story is being told, whether real or fictitious, and suggests with whatever shade of conviction that its events actually occurred, or something like them. It probably accounts for more than nine-tenths of fiction, dialogue apart. It accounts, almost of necessity, for the greater part of the memoir-novel and its Victorian and later imitations, except that

> (a) the conclusions of such novels may draw us at last into the present: 'And here resolving to harass myself no more', as *Robinson Crusoe* ends, 'I am preparing for a longer journey than all these . . .', as the narrator-hero makes ready for death; and
> (b) the author or 'editor' may intervene in his own person, in the present tense.

Letter-novels too are largely, if less decisively, in the past tense, being mainly concerned with events that have recently occurred. And the third-person novel since 1800 has commonly been in the past, as if acknowledging its ancestry in epic and romance, as well as in memoirs and letters; and subject on the whole only to those exceptions already remarked on: dialogue, conclusions and the occasional authorial voice. The occasional drop into the present now marks a special, and often ironic, effect. But the use of free indirect style can make for subtle confusions here: past tense used in a manner the reader is often, but not always, asked to translate into the present. 'And of course he was coming to her party tonight', Virginia Woolf's Mrs Dalloway remarks to herself, where the conjoining of 'was' and 'tonight' is ungrammatical on any supposition but that of *style indirect libre.*

2. *Present.* Damon Runyon is perhaps the only author of note to cast his fiction mainly in the present tense, as in *Guys and Dolls* (1932); but there are isolated instances elsewhere, such as Michel Butor's *La Modification* (1957), which has the additional singularity of being in the second person (*vous*). Oddly enough, the present tense does not usually prevail in stream-of-consciousness novels. Joyce's *Portrait of the Artist* (1916) is an autobiographical novel in the third person and past tense, the tense being justified by the fact that it is recollection; his *Ulysses* (1922) too is framed in the past, and so is Proust's great novel.

Outside dialogue and authorial voice, the present tense is always exceptional in fiction, and without a continuous tradition. That is not because it is too radical but because, surprisingly, it is not radical enough. It is a little like playing *Hamlet* in modern dress: the onlooker soon ceases to notice.

3. *Mixed tense*, as in Malcolm Bradbury's *The History Man* (1975), which is essentially recounted in the present tense, but with long insertions composed in the past tense to mark events earlier than the main narrative. That amounts to the technique of flashback, the simplest instance of mixture. Others can be more elaborate. Dickens's *Bleak House* (1853) is the classic in English, and still the most daring and original instance: a first-person narrative by the heroine largely in the past tense, retelling her experiences – interspersed with chapters in the present, in a vatic style learned from Carlyle's *French Revolution* (1837), where events are viewed omnisciently as by an historian.

The nearest source to that audacious device can only have given Dickens an inkling of such an idea: the late memoir-novel of mixed tense, like James Hogg's *Confessions of a Justified Sinner* (1824), where the narrator's account and the editor's are offered without intermixture; or Mary Shelley's *Frankenstein* (1818). A modern equivalent is Faulkner's *As I Lay Dying* (1930).

★

TIME

What is the time described by the classic novel? I shall consider present, past and remembered time here, accepting that science fiction, and novels about the future in general, like Aldous Huxley's *Brave New World* (1932) or Angus Wilson's *The Old Man at the Zoo* (1961), lack a continuous life before the present century.

1. *Time present*, or so nearly present as to make no qualitative difference to life as it is lived. Trollope's title *The Way We Live Now* (1875) sums up to perfection the claims of this class of fiction.

Some may think it a powerful tribute to the potency of the past tense as conventional to narrative that novels such as these preserve it no less consistently than historical novels. But it might be simpler, and less ingenious, to see the tense of such novels as the literary equivalent of gossip. One naturally uses the past tense, in life, to describe something that happened an hour a week ago. All Jane

Austen's six novels fall within this class, as does by far the greater part of eighteenth-century fiction before her. And so, to indulge a broad impression, does much the greater part of twentieth-century fiction. It is only in the century between Scott's *Waverley* and the First World War, or 1814–1914, that Time Present loses its easy predominance.

The demands of accuracy, it is tempting to suppose, are nowhere higher than in Time Present, and nowhere harder to meet. That argument, on reflection, is perhaps tempting rather than convincing. Do we really know our own times, for this purpose, better than we know past ages? The claim needs to be seen in practical terms. However much a reader may know about the world he lives in, he may rightly feel himself dangerously ignorant of it, in the plain sense of finding difficulties in living efficiently in it; whereas his ignorance about the ancient Carthage of Flaubert, or George Eliot's Florence, though vaster, may inconvenience him less. How much do we really know of other professions in our own age and country, or of other regions in our own nation? The social novelist, above all kinds of novelist, is subject to the demand of accuracy. But that demand is only doubtfully more exacting in novels about the present age.

Time Present, for all that, confronts the novelist with a demand for exceptionally subtle discriminations. There are areas of judgement well within the common domain here, and he had better get them right. All that is especially true in the realm of manners, where the response of word or gesture is a matter so finely calibrated, and so susceptible to alteration year by year, that the creator of fiction sometimes needs to proffer his credentials to a reader who is equally qualified to judge. 'This little work was finished in the year 1803', Jane Austen wrote in 1816, in her prefatory Advertisement to *Northanger Abbey*, 'and was intended for immediate publication'; but failing to appear then, 'some observation is necessary upon those parts of the work which thirteen years have made comparatively obsolete'. Thirteen years is less than an epoch. But in 1803 England was re-entering the war against Napoleonic France, and by 1816 peace had come, something of importance in human behaviour having changed too: 'During that period, places, manners, books and opinions have undergone considerable changes.' The apology shows her claim to chronicle the present to have been deliberately analytic.

By Victorian times it is a critic's commonplace to urge one novelist against another as a more accurate record of present times. James Bryce complained as an historian in his *Studies in Contemporary*

Biography (1903) that Dickens's conception of lower middle-class existence in London had failed to grow since the 1830s, when he was a young reporter, and that the twentieth century would be better advised to study Trollope to gain a true sense of the England of the 1850s and 1860s; adding that life had changed again since then.

2. *Time past*, or historical time. History is a matter of documents, and it grows backwards from that point in the recent past where recollection and hearsay cease to count for much. There is an interesting border zone here, where the historian or antiquary seeks out the survivors of an all-but-vanished age to fill out his knowledge of a world largely known from manuscripts and books. Scott, who set on foot a nineteenth-century European vogue for historical fiction with *Waverley*, describes in a postscript how he had met Jacobites in his youth, and heard speak of the Forty-Five 'from those who were actors' in that rising, though that event occurred a quarter of a century before his own birth in 1771: 'Indeed, the most romantic parts of this narrative are precisely those which have a foundation in fact.' This assertion is repeated, even strengthened, in his general preface to the Waverley novels in 1829, only three years before his death:

> I had been a good deal in the Highlands at a time when they were much less accessible, and much less visited, than they have been of late years, and was acquainted with many of the old warriors of 1745. · · ·

But with all his passion for documents, Scott's attitude to historical accuracy could be cavalier, especially when challenged. It would be as absurd, he remarks in a preface to *Ivanhoe* (1820), which is set in twelfth-century England, to 'pretend to the observation of complete accuracy,' whether in costume, language or manners, as it would be to write dialogue in Anglo-Saxon or Norman French, or to print in blackletter like Caxton. In an impish note to a later edition, he approvingly quotes a remark by his friend the Gothic novelist 'Monk' Lewis that he had made a slave black purely as a matter of artistic contrast: 'Could he have derived a similar advantage from making his heroine blue, blue she should have been.' In *Kenilworth* (1821), similarly, he introduces Shakespeare (ch. 17) as a grown actor and poet into events of 1575, when, as he must have known, Shakespeare was only eleven years old.

But such flagrant disregard for detail need not obscure Scott's triumphs as an historical innovator. His greatest innovation lies in grasping personality as an index of a place and time. The figure of the 'Chevalier', or Bonnie Prince Charlie, in the fortieth chapter of *Waverley*, where the brilliant young prince at a ball in Holyroodhouse captivates the young Hanoverian hero against his will, 'unaccustomed to the address and manners of a polished court' – all this is an imaginative stroke that transforms historiography as well as fiction for an era to come. 'No master of ceremonies is necessary to present a Waverley to a Stuart', says the Chevalier, extending his hand; and then follow the words that bring Waverley to his knees:

'If Mr Waverley should . . . determine to embrace a cause which has little to recommend it but its justice, and follow a prince who throws himself upon the affections of his people, to recover the throne of his ancestors or perish in the attempt, I can only say that among these nobles and gentlemen he will find worthy associates in a gallant enterprise, and will follow a master who may be unfortunate but, I trust, will never be ungrateful.'

The reader knows that the Chevalier neither recovered the throne nor perished in the attempt, so that the scene is as much a finely balanced act of loyalty to the House of Hanover as a romantic fanfare for a lost cause. Scott, himself a Hanoverian and a Unionist, always shows the generosity of the victor. But in all Europe no novelist had so succeeded in distilling the essence of a civilisation and a cause into a character, or endowing that cause with fit speech, before this book. Balzac was to write enthusiastically of his master's gift for turning the general into the specific (*'particulariser des généralités'*), in contrast to his many imitators, who merely generalised upon a single detail.

The historical novel is a kind of novel first, a kind of history only second. At its most historical it can tell of protagonists, events and settings that are all recorded in history, as in Robert Graves's *I, Claudius* (1934) – a fairly recent phenomenon. Or it can set imaginary events in real settings, and with allusions, or something more, to real historical personages – the classic mode from Mme de La Fayette to Scott and Thackeray. (The story of Mme de La Fayette's *La Princesse de Clèves* [1678] is imaginary, though her knowledge of sixteenth-century France was real; and the Waverley novels mix historical characters like Prince Charles Stuart with others that are pure invention, like Captain Waverley.) Or it can, at its novelistic extreme, use history only as a backdrop and exclude historical characters, as Georgette Heyer does in her novels about a romantic eighteenth century.

There are many gradations. But a point somewhere near the middle, as in Scott, is surely the most strategic here, where some characters are historical in a plain sense, others in a symbolic: carrying, like Captain Waverley, the burden of an historical choice in their minds and conduct.

Yet the historical novel is still a kind of history as well as a kind of novel, and its finest monuments have inevitably suffered from the advance of history itself. No one now reads *Waverley* to learn of the Forty-Five, though they might do worse. The high vogue of this species of fiction was so brief, and is now so remote, at least in England, that it is hard now to recapture its sense of intellectual purpose. As a predominating form it lasted from *Waverley* to Thackeray's *Henry Esmond*, which was felt in its sustained pastiche to have set an unattainably high ideal, or from 1814 to 1852. Its minor luminaries in England are Harrison Ainsworth and Bulwer Lytton; its far greater continental exponents are Manzoni, the Flaubert of *Salammbô*, and the Tolstoy of *War and Peace*. Its twentieth-century outposts, though numerous, are not often of the first rank, though there are occasional masterpieces like Marguerite Yourcenar's *Mémoires d'Hadrien* (1951) or Lampedusa's *Il gattopardo* (1958). The trouble is that we no longer turn first to fiction to learn history. That is because we no longer believe Scott when he says that romance has its foundation in fact, or no longer think that claim to be enough.

3. *Time remembered*, a phrase reminiscent of Proust, whose kingdom this is, though he calls it lost. Remembered time lies between the present and the historical. It is what we recall for ourselves; or what we recollect parents, or grandparents, or their contemporaries speaking of when we were ourselves young. This is the domain of George Eliot's *Adam Bede, Silas Marner* and *Middlemarch*, all set earlier in her own century; and though it does not so clearly predominate in Dickens, it must still be supposed his favourite ground, since his mind drifts towards it almost without willing it to be there.

This is the most Victorian of all points in time. Scott had already bordered on it; and Maria Edgeworth had approached it in *Castle Rackrent* (1800), set in the bad old days in Ireland before the Independency of 1782. But then that little novel must have been designed largely for those who knew little or nothing of rural Ireland in any period, so that it does not possess the essential quality of shared experience that animates *The Pickwick Papers* or *Adam Bede*. Time Remembered is above all an exercise in nostalgia. Charlotte Brontë opens *Shirley* (1849) with a dismissal of 'late' and 'present' years as 'dusty, sunburnt, hot, arid', and announces: 'We are going back to the beginning of this century.' In its first paragraph, *Adam Bede* proposes the year of its beginning as 1799. *Pickwick* is set in the stage-coach England of Dickens's boyhood, without passenger railways – earlier than 1830, then; its opening is firmly dated 1827, when Dickens was fifteen, and it is to the 1820s, or pre-Victorian England, that his imagination resistlessly returns. He wrote only two historical novels, *Barnaby Rudge* and *A Tale of Two Cities*; and his handling of time present, as in *Our Mutual Friend*, sometimes suggests he shared the Brontë view that it was dusty and arid. 'It was old London bridge in those days', he remarks nostalgically in *Great Expectations* (ch. 46); and that bridge, as the reader is meant to recall, was replaced by a new one in the late 1820s. Thackeray's *Vanity Fair* is placed at a similarly enticing distance from the reality it describes: in 1848 there would be plenty of readers to remember Waterloo, and plenty more who could recall hearing it talked of. Thirty years, give or take a decade, is about perfection for Time Remembered.

Its heyday was mid-Victorian. The great exception is Trollope who, from his first success with *The Warden* in 1855, preferred the present. But George Eliot favours remembered time, though not consistently; and Thomas Hardy writes mainly within it, often using his novels to convey information of a barely familiar, and sometimes barely credible kind, like the wife-selling episode in the first chapter of *The Mayor of Casterbridge* (1886). But the element of shared recollection, being regionally distanced, is evidently weaker here. With his last novel, *Jude the Obscure* (1896), he moved to the present, as George Eliot had done with hers, *Daniel Deronda* (1876).

By Joyce and Proust, in the new century, a fiction lies wholly within the framework of memory, and the technique called stream of consciousness is perhaps best seen as the final stage of Remembered Time. But by now the demands placed upon the power of private recollection are so absolute as to end in renunciation: an escape into language-consciousness, in the case of Joyce, with *Finnegans Wake* (1939); in the case of Proust, in the last pages of *A la recherche du temps perdu* (1913–27), with a Wordsworthian intuition that memory is forever imperfect, since the remembrancer is always a being other than the youth he endeavours to remember: 'We occupy a place in Time which is perpetually augmented', he remarks, comparing himself in exquisite despair to a man on high stilts, so high that he can hardly see the ground beneath him: 'I may be too weak to maintain my hold upon a past so far beneath me.' To capitalise the word *Temps*, as he does, is to cast doubts upon its traditional instrumentality as something through which the novelist can voyage easily, recapturing itself as it once was. Proust's Time is lost, *perdu*, and no search or research can altogether recover it, though it recovers much as it tries.

Time Remembered fades out of our classic fiction, then, dying by a sort of excess. Its more recent attempts are less ambitious: Evelyn Waugh's trilogy of the Second World War, *Sword of Honour* (1952–61); or Richard Hughes's unfinished trilogy *The Human Predicament*, only two novels long: *The Fox in the Attic* (1961) and *The Wooden Shepherdess* (1973), set in the earlier years of the century. Compared with the passionate concern of the Victorians for the life of their parents and their fading rural cultures, all this looks pale and uninvolved. The Industrial Revolution offered an ideal opportunity to Time Remembered, when memory could cherish an event, or a remark, from a social system still near in time but astonishingly different from the present. It is the quiet contemplation of memory that counts here. George Eliot, in a letter, speaks of long holding 'the germ' of *Adam Bede* in her mind, a real incident of village child murder 'for years on years, as a dead germ, apparently – till time had made my mind a nidus in which it could fructify' (7 October 1859).

MENTAL TIME

Being obsequious to the imagination, time might be thought obedient to the novelist too. And yet most novelists have been content to remain its willing slaves. It is odd they have imposed their will so little. The strength of a story is still felt to be chronological, and most readers still demand development, preferring a novel to move steadily forward than to recoil or zigzag.

To this day, then, most novels are a matter of one thing after another, like life itself. But some novelists have long since seen that Mental Time, or the time in which we live our own thoughts, is not the same as what is measured by the clock. Any fresh experience, like travel, stretches time out; and obsession can take one out of clock time altogether, for moments or hours, as ideas associate in patterns more intricate, and less conscious, than the formal or the rational. That perception can be studied in Locke's *Essay* (1690), which Sterne in *Tristram Shandy* admiringly called 'a history-book . . . of what passes in a man's own mind' (II, 2). It is enacted in the novel itself. Tristram's father Walter Shandy and his brother Toby wait two hours and ten minutes by the clock for Tristram's birth, 'but it seems an age' (III, 18), and Uncle Toby, a man of hobbies, only recovers his proper sense of time when he falls in love with Widow Wadman.

The most compelling instances of mental time in our fiction might be expected in the novels of Joyce and Virginia Woolf, where mental acts predominate over the physical. But mental acts lose much of their sense of distinction when they cease to be governed by the reality around them, or cease even to try to govern it. That must be among the reasons why the stream of consciousness, far from enriching or dignifying a sense of mind, impoverished it so quickly and died so soon. It flourished only for a quarter of a century, between the appearance of Proust's first novel in 1913 and the last fictions of Woolf and Joyce in the 1930s.

To be felt to be out of time, or in a time of one's own, there needs to be a real time to be out of. That is what makes Dickens's Mr Dorrit an unforgettable and infinitely pathetic figure, as he lives rich and free and yet ever mindful of his prison life; or Dr Manette in *A Tale of Two Cities*, who after eighteen years in the Bastille can still revert to his penal task of cobbling shoes, though in the freedom of London. 'I believe', he explains to his confidante, sharing the security of the third person in an account of his own symptoms,

> that there had been a strong and extraordinary revival of the train of thought and remembrance that was the first cause of the malady. Some intense associations of the most distressing nature were vividly recalled, I think. It is probable that there had long been a dread lurking in his mind, that those associations would be recalled − say, under certain circumstances − say, on a particular occasion. . . . (II, 19)

with no power of recall over what had happened during the relapse. The notion that men make their own time is familiar to Dickens, as it had been to Sterne a century before him. But it is no matter for rejoicing there. Better the tyranny of the clock than the remorseless and irrational power of memory over its victims and its thralls.

8 *History in its Place*

The novel measures itself against history, if only because it is so often in the past tense, and so often chronological. Truth, as Shaftesbury noted archly in his *Characteristicks* (1711), 'is the most powerful thing in the world, since even fiction itself must be governed by it' (I, 4). But the demand for truth was a trial as well as a challenge to the novel in the seventeenth and eighteenth centuries, and historical falsehood was only one of the several damaging imputations it had to meet. The critical dignity of fiction, a matter now seemingly taken for granted by all who are not professional critics, was once hard fought and hard won.

★

Three objections were commonly levelled. First, the novel was not a classical *genre*, being sanctioned neither by Aristotle nor by any Renaissance critic. It is significant that Samuel Johnson never wrote about a novel or novelist, though Boswell shows how ready he was to talk about them. Fielding had tried to meet this objection in his prefaces to *Joseph Andrews* (1742), offering his novel as a 'comic epic in prose'; but there is not much evidence that his formula was seriously regarded by many of his own countrymen in that century. This is an issue that was talked out rather than solved: the problem of classification on classical lines, active before 1800, did not last, and the claim since then has more usually been to an excellence pure and simple. Jane Austen, in an uncharacteristic outburst in *Northanger Abbey* (1818), exclaimed angrily against the phrase 'It is only a novel', and indignantly instanced works by Fanny Burney and Maria Edgeworth:

> ... only some work in which the greatest powers of the mind are
> displayed, in which the most thorough knowledge of human na-

ture, the happiest delineation of its varieties, the liveliest effusions of wit and humour, are conveyed to the world in the best chosen language (ch. 5).

That spirited defence was already earned. But it is notable that Jane Austen does not attempt to fit the novel in any wider generic scheme here, or acknowledge the attempt of anyone else to do so. It is enough for her that it is well written and accurate to life.

Again, the novel was not true. Fielding laboured here too, to establish his novels as a species of biography; but the claim was too facetiously made to be seriously heard. It was an uncommon critical claim for fiction before 1800 that upheld its power as information, as distinct from moral enlightenment. The Waverley novels were to make that claim good, and young Victorians could be encouraged to read them to acquire a knowledge of history. But that is not a widespread eighteenth-century educational sentiment, even though historical novels existed earlier than Scott.

And finally, the novel could be thought immoral, like the romances that had gone before it. Bunyan had condemned 'beastly romances' in *Mr Badman* (1680), complaining that they 'set all fleshly lusts on fire'. Richardson's programme was to fight one fire with another, providing fictions that could safely, even beneficially, be placed in the hands of young persons to save them from worse. That programme was announced on his title-pages and in his prefaces; and though it had predecessors, it seems to have imposed itself on its age as a remarkable undertaking. Diderot, in his essay 'Eloge de Richardson' (1761), begins by remarking that hitherto a novel has meant 'a tissue of imaginary and frivolous adventures, the reading of which was dangerous to taste and morals', and acclaims Richardson as the successor of such great moralists as Montaigne and La Rochefoucauld. A low view of the species lingered on, in spite of all this strenuous advocacy, and Trollope in his *Autobiography* (1883) speaks of an 'embargo' on the unrestricted reading of novels among respectable families in his youth, in the 1820s, though he remarks that it had been lifted by the 1870s (ch. 12). To this day, for all that, there are those who would think it wrong to read a novel in the morning.

The need to find a literary place for the novel faded, at least in neoclassical terms, and the argument about its morality grew confused, as such arguments often do, losing itself in a welter of considerations and counter-considerations. (Is virtue best taught by concealing vices or by denouncing them?) The argument for and against descriptive truth, however, is still alive. To this day there are heated controversies claiming or denying the power of fiction to describe, or describe accurately, how things are or how they once were.

The extreme version of the descriptive case, or realism, arose as a term of literary debate in the France of the 1820s and 1830s as a proposal for *'la littérature du vrai'*, and flourished in the mid- and late-nineteenth century, in Flaubert, George Eliot, Turgenev and Fontane. Its contrary is any doctrine that doubts or denies that descriptive power, whether as a duty or as a possibility: *Tristram Shandy* occupies such a position; and so, with a solemnity that could not have failed to amuse Sterne, had he known it, does the *Nouvelle Critique* of the Paris of the 1960s. Romance is not its contrary, since life, as Scott pointed out, can be as romantic as any fiction.

The novel has defended itself in three broadly distinct ways as a descriptive mode against the charge of untruth.

1. It has itself pretended to be history, as the memoir-novel often pretends to be a real memoir, or a letter-novel a genuine collection of letters. That pretence is of variable force. Richardson, in his letter on *Clarissa*, had proclaimed that he did not want it to be thought literally genuine – only to 'avoid hurting that kind of historical faith which fiction itself is generally read with ...' (19 April 1748). That is a milder claim than was made by some of his contemporaries. Prévost, in his preface to *Cleveland* (1731), a novel about an imaginary bastard of Oliver Cromwell, claims to have had the original from Cromwell's son in London, who let him copy out the manuscript memoir and translate it 'in a form suitable for today' (*'sous la forme sous laquelle elle peut paraître aujourd'hui'*). Such claims could seriously deceive: Steele, in a *Tatler* paper of 1709, warns against

> some merry gentlemen of the French nation, who have written very advantageous histories of their exploits in war, love and politics, under the title of memoirs. . . . I do here give notice to all book-sellers and translators whatsoever that the word 'Memoir' is French for a novel; and do require of them that they sell and translate it accordingly. (no. 84)

Given that English has two words for *'histoire'* – 'story' and 'history' – this is a more reasonable demand in English than in French, but it was not met. Fielding loves to equivocate with 'history' and 'biography' in his prefaces and elsewhere, and many novelists before 1800 thought the confusion something to enjoy rather than to clarify. Many of the first readers of *Crusoe* must have thought it an authentic document; others must have wished it were so.

2. The novel could claim a new and distinct dignity of its own, as fiction, of which Fielding's formula 'the comic epic in prose' is an instance. It is the unequivocal claim, explicit or not, of fiction in the nineteenth. Jane Austen's outburst about 'the most thorough knowledge of human nature' is a clear signal of that new dignity; much clearer than Maria Edgeworth, whom she admired, her senior by some seven years, who can spatter her fictions with annotations like 'Fact' that make her fictions disturbingly unclear in the status they claim for themselves. But then a Jane Austen novel, lacking as it commonly does either preface, commentary, glossary, or even (with rare exceptions) an authorial voice, is remarkable as a seamless web of fiction from which no exit is offered but its own last chapter. Scott, who jokes with his reader, as Dickens and Thackeray do, is far less consistent than that; and Peacock is not interested in that kind of consistency at all. If a pioneer must be named among the famous in fictional dignity of this innovative kind, then the name had best be Miss Austen's. Henry James claimed it for her in 'The Lesson of Balzac' (1905), though if James had known as much about the history of technique as about its modern practice he would have seen more deliberation in her art than he did.

> Jane Austen, with all her light felicity, leaves us hardly more curious of her process, or of the experience in her that fed it, than the brown thrush who tells his story from the garden bough . . . . A short sharp cut, one of the sharpest and shortest achieved, in this field, by the general judgement, came out, betimes, straight at her feet.

James even dares speak of her 'dropped stitches' later mistaken for masterstrokes. But there are few dropped stitches in those six novels of hers: nothing much left even for James to pick up.

3. The novel might claim a new dignity as history. This has nothing to do with the deliberate confusions of Defoe, Prévost or Richardson: it is a claim not to factual truth, but to interpretative skills of a kind offered by professional historians. James, in the same Balzac essay, rudely calls Macaulay the 'first slightly ponderous amoroso' of Jane Austen, meaning merely that Macaulay was the first critic of note, so far as he knew, to have acclaimed her. But the point is more profound

than he supposed. Macaulay's essays, and his *History of England*, are distinguished precisely in their sense of human character: they perceive how motive and personality, the inside and the outside of an historic figure like Chatham or William III, work together to make a man. That is a perception to which the novel had massively contributed. Under the influence of the very history it had helped to create, it was to contribute more. When Joseph Conrad died in 1924, his friend and collaborator Ford Madox Ford, in his preface to *Conrad: A Personal Remembrance* (1924), recorded a conviction they had long shared, that

> a novel should be the biography of a man or of an affair, and a biography whether of a man or of an affair should be a novel: both being, if they are efficiently performed, renderings of such affairs as are our human lives.

This suggests an interpenetrative influence, even a merging, of fact and fiction under the name of history.

★

The new historical dignity of fiction heralded by Scott had begun in a sense of place as well as of time, and the regional and the historical are so interwoven here as to be almost one.

A regional novel has two defining characteristics. One is that the place where it is set should be felt as a pervading presence, in its manners and even in its dialect: as Rousseau's *La Nouvelle Héloïse* (1761) is set in the pays de Vaud, in Switzerland, or Mme de Charrière's *Lettres neuchâteloises* (1784), written by a Dutchwoman who was Swiss by marriage, is set in a Swiss canton to the north of Rousseau's. Both use occasional dialect words, usually explained, and details about local habits such as foods and wine-making. Maria Edgeworth's *Castle Rackrent* (1800) is a more radical instance, being itself composed in an Irish dialect, discreetly normalised and with editorial explanations.

The other characteristic is that such regional information should be offered as distinct from what the reader is likely to know, and to that extent surprising. That is why, in the nature of things, a novel about London or Paris cannot qualify, unless it is about some odd quarter or corner unknown to polite readers. Since readers are assumed to be metropolitan and sophisticated, odd here can only mean poor. You can tell Mayfair about Stepney, in such a novel, but not Stepney about Mayfair. Scott struck the right note of surprise in *Waverley*, reporting on clan wars in the Highlands:

> It seemed like a dream to Waverley that these deeds of violence should be familiar to men's minds, and currently talked of as falling within the common order of things, and happening daily in the immediate vicinity, without his having crossed the seas, and while he was yet in the otherwise well-ordered island of Great Britain. (ch. 15)

A place is also a time, and to this day a region can be felt to represent an era. A Parisian in Auvergne, or a Londoner in rural Wales or Scotland, can feel himself to have shed years or decades in fashions of life, and can recall a world he knew in childhood, or of which he heard his parents speak. A train or plane can perform like a time-machine. All that represents the large perception of Rousseau and Maria Edgeworth in the years before 1800. *Rackrent* was written in the 1790s by a young woman who, under her father's influence, had passed through a period of interest in Rousseau, and the novel sought to inform a sophisticated public about the remote life of County Longford before the Independency that had established the sovereignty of the Irish Parliament: *an Hibernian tale*, as the subtitle has it, *taken from facts, and from the manners of the Irish squires before the year 1782*. Scott, already an established poet, began writing *Waverley* several years after, thinking that the 'admirable Irish portraits drawn by Miss Edgeworth' might be imitated in a novel about Scotland. The claims he makes for his own, in 'A Postscript which should have been a Preface', echo hers in perceiving the link between place and time. The past can only be studied now region by region: history put in its place. 'There is no European nation', Scott exaggeratingly remarks, which

> within the course of half a century, or little more, has undergone so complete a change as this kingdom of Scotland. The effects of the insurrection of 1745 – the destruction of the patriarchal power of the Highland chiefs – the abolition of the heritable jurisdictions of the Lowland nobility and barons – the total eradication of the Jacobite party which, averse to intermingle with the English, or

adopt their customs, long continued to pride themselves upon maintaining ancient Scottish manners and customs – commenced this innovation.

And yet the change, though massive, had been gradual, and less like a revolution and restoration than the motion of a stream: 'We are not aware of the progress we have made until we fix our eye on the now distant point from which we have drifted.' The novel is based upon documentation as well as talk, and it does what history is supposed to do, creating a credible picture of a lost world.

The immediate object of the regional could be twofold: to educate the metropolis in the ways of a region, in an age of advancing national consciousness; and to capture and fix a fleeting past, and one perhaps neglected by professional historians, before it had forever fled. There is some evidence it succeeded in both these objects, if imperfectly. George III is reported to have read *Rackrent* as soon as it appeared, to have rubbed his hands appreciatively and remarked: 'What, what! I know something now of my Irish subjects' – mistaking it, like many since, for a contemporary portrait. The Waverley novels undoubtedly fed a passion for the Highlands that left so strong a mark on the Victorian mind, including its Queen's. The rural Yorkshire of the Brontë sisters, and the West Country of Thomas Hardy, elevated those regions into the arena of polite discussion and literary pilgrimage. And it is equally certain that the regional novel has acted as an historical preservative, stimulating local history in its wake. Village tradition, Hardy wrote to Rider Haggard in March 1902, or that 'vast mass of unwritten folk-lore, local chronicle, local topography, and nomenclature – is absolutely sinking, has nearly sunk, into eternal oblivion'. The Wessex novels were written to compensate for that loss. So was Lampedusa's *Il gattopardo* (1958), a belated triumph in the Scott tradition written by a Sicilian landowner to recall and preserve the life of his province a century earlier, during the events of the Risorgimento of 1860. He wrote it, so his widow tells, to console himself over the destruction of his beloved country home by the Allies in the occupation of 1943.

★

A map of the British Isles might be sprinkled with dates to represent the progress of regional fiction in English. 1800 would have to be planted in the middle of Ireland, in a region little known even to the Irish; 1814 in the Scottish Highlands, for *Waverley*; and 1847 in West Yorkshire, for *Wuthering Heights* and *Jane Eyre*. The sudden outburst of the industrial novel, brief as it was, had already begun: 1845–8 in and about Manchester for Disraeli's *Sybil* and Elizabeth Gaskell's *Mary Barton*; 1854 for Dickens's *Hard Times*; and 1859–61 in Warwickshire for George Eliot's early Midland fiction, *Adam Bede*, *Mill on the Floss* and *Silas Marner*. Then, in the 1870s, comes Hardy's West Country or 'Wessex', and the map soon grows too crowded for easy use.

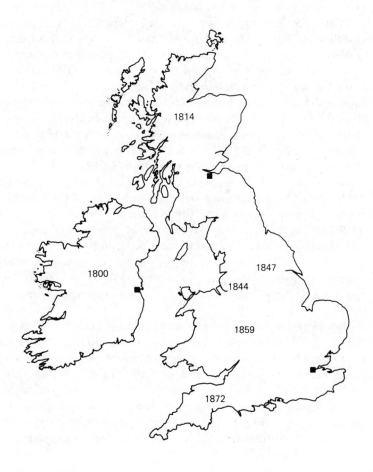

A region, for this purpose, can be a city or part of one, like Arthur Morrison's *A Child of the Jago* (1896) on the London slums, or Joyce's Dublin in *Portrait of the Artist* (1916), or Alfred Döblin's *Alexanderplatz* (1929) on the loneliness of Berlin. There now seems no reason why this progress should ever stop: by 1900 it had even ceased to limit itself to a single nation. Expatriates could turn its techniques towards informing a motherland about its imperial responsibilities or the lives of backward peoples. Kipling's *Kim* (1900) is heavily based on a childhood recollection of India, Conrad's *Nostromo* (1904) on the briefest of visits to South America, and D. H. Lawrence's *Plumed Serpent* (1926) on a short stay in Mexico. The process set on foot by an Irish spinster and her Scottish pupil approaches the miracle of perpetual motion.

That movement is from outer to inner, taking London as its centre, and then out again. The pattern would become clearer if our map of the British Isles could be mentally extended into a map of the world. It starts in wild and remote places: in an Ireland far from Dublin, a Scotland that is not Edinburgh or Glasgow, and a Yorkshire and Lancashire as remote from polite imaginings as another planet. 'Rightly understood', Disraeli admonishes his reader in *Coningsby*, 'Manchester is as great a human exploit as Athens' (IV, i), and he makes it sound as difficult to reach. Then the movement draws inwards towards the metropolis, with the West Midlands of George Eliot and later Arnold Bennett, the Wessex of Hardy and the East Midlands of Lawrence. But well before the end of the nineteenth century, the movement outwards has already begun. In 1823–41, with his Leatherstocking novels, James Fenimore Cooper, the American Scott, took the tale to the American frontier, and before Disraeli or the Brontës wrote. George Sand was writing of provincial France in the 1840s, Turgenev of provincial Russia before 1850, and Gottfried Keller's *Der grüne Heinrich*, on rural Switzerland, appeared in 1854.

By the 1890s the movement outwards embraces the world, with Kipling and Conrad; and from the 1870s onwards Henry James turns it to new advantage with the international theme, soon followed by E. M. Forster: Europe contrasted with America, Italy with England, and in Forster's *A Passage to India* (1924) India with the English. Forster's last novel, and his greatest, is as delicate a triumph as the regional spirit could hope to win in fiction, though by now the notion of a region has widened to signify nations and whole peoples. It is a very English novel, and about the English, though set some thousands of miles outside the adventuring civilisation it depicts.

★

History needs research, and that can be true of historical fiction too. Maria Edgeworth did not need to pursue her 'facts', as she loves to call them, since she knew them already from observation or hearsay. But Scott, though he could talk flippantly about the claims of accuracy, is plainly a learned man in his fiction, an amateur passion for border ballads and other records extending from the later Middle ages down into the Scotland of the seventeenth and eighteenth centuries. At the age of fifteen, as he tells in the 1829 preface to *Waverley*, he fell ill, and was driven into 'becoming a glutton for books', reading everything the Edinburgh circulating library could provide in 'romances, old plays and epic poetry', so that his boyish mind was 'unconsciously amassing materials for the task in which it has been my lot to be so much employed'. It was an education for a lifetime.

The record after Scott is variable; but for half a century and more, the tendency advanced towards a scholarly interpretation of the novelist's duty. In the first half of the century, research is exceptional. The Brontës usually drew their regional knowledge from what they had seen and heard, though Charlotte sent for copies of the *Leeds Mercury* for 1812–14 when she was writing *Shirley* (1849). Disraeli was a clever listener who sometimes over-estimated his own powers of subterfuge: one is not supposed to guess from the opening chapters of *Coningsby* (1844) that the author was not himself an Etonian, or a pupil at any other school of note. Sometimes there are convenient short cuts to knowledge. The elder Dumas had only dreamed of imitating Scott in French, until one day he met a young professor of history eager to make money, and was supplied with historical facts on the France of Louis XIII out of which, along with a memoir supposedly by d'Artagnan, he wrote *Les Trois Mousquetaires* (1844). But after 1850 the pace becomes more exacting, for some. Flaubert, George Eliot and Zola do much of their own scholarly preparation, and their novels sometimes smell of the notebook; indeed the notes for *Middlemarch*, detailing the events of 1829–32 after some forty years, and garnering up little fragments of knowledge from *The Times* for those years, still survive in the library of Harvard.

The high point of such research is from the 1850s to the end of the century, and it fades as an historical method after the death of Zola in 1902. The new truths for the new century are psychological rather than documentary or archival. Henry James kept notebooks from 1878, but they represent his musings and occasional observations rather than research. The novel does not step out of history, but it largely steps out of historiography, and grows less interested in what historians write. In Joyce, Proust and Virginia Woolf fiction remains rooted in a specific time and place, and a time and place one is meant to recognise. But they are not inspired by that passion for historical knowledge that Scott and Flaubert had once known.

★

Has fictional history taught men much about the human past? For the moment, at least, its instructive powers are sometimes felt to be paltry, and professional historians nowadays rarely pay it even the most modest tribute. Few enough now read novels with the purpose of learning history, unless in childhood. Nor has the historical mode usually attracted the most ambitious talents in fiction since the First World War. The historical novel lives, undoubtedly. It is even numerous, on a head count. What is more, it has its notable instances, like R. C. Hutchinson's *Testament* (1938) on the Russian Revolution, and Solzhenitsyn's *August 1914* (1971) on the events that led to it, as well as J. G. Farrell's *Siege of Krishnapur* (1973) on the Indian Mutiny. But it is hard now to imagine a scholar or statesman venerating fiction of this sort, as Gladstone once venerated Scott. An enormous critique by his friend Lord Acton of Shorthouse's *John Inglesant*, written as a letter to the Prime Minister's daughter in March 1882, soon after the novel appeared, shows what such books could once signify to men of affairs: Acton calls it the most 'thoughtful and suggestive' work to appear since *Middlemarch*, though as a professional historian he painstakingly lists its numerous factual errors on the seventeenth century. Nowadays they would hardly rate as errors, in a way a scholar might feel to be important, and it would be hard to imagine an historian troubling to list them.

But it is possible that the weightiest influences here are ones that remain silent and unacknowledged. There is the effect of historical fiction on history itself. The grand difference between Macaulay and Gibbon, it has been said, lies in the Waverley novels, which fall halfway between; and that difference lies in Scott's perception of two far-reaching truths. The first is anthropological: that common humanity is a limiting assumption in history, since place and time count powerfully as well, and that what divides mankind into tribes and nations may be as interesting as what mankind possesses in common. The other is that it is possible to see a society as a totality, from top to bottom, and not to confine oneself to a fragment of it like Jane Austen's famous 'small piece of ivory': to see how its ranks and classes contrive to live together, and fit together.

In 1811 Scott drew out of his lower drawer the first chapters of *Waverley*, which he had abandoned some six years before on the advice of a friend, and took up the story near the point where Captain Waverley enters the Highland village of Tully-Veolan and views its miserable inhabitants of naked children, tired old men and all too lively dogs, and wanders up the drive of a country house, handing his horse to a servant and knocking on a hall door marked 1594, to find himself ushered into a feudal world where his host quotes Latin and the daughter plays the piano and reads Italian. European fiction has not recovered from that moment of insight, and never can. What Scott perceived was that time and place are ultimately indistinguishable, remote regions embodying a past that great cities have lost and may yet be taught to envy.

The historical vision is above all one that can see how all the circumstances of a world, both physical and mental, can hang together, achieving a coherence that is at once eccentric to the eye of the onlooker and yet imposing. That is why Scott's hero is an observer and a far traveller. He is the proverbial onlooker who sees most of the game. Stand outside a world like the Jacobite Highlands and observe it, so Scott suggests, and its tragic error of dynastic judgement is consistent with everything it believed and was. Its longing for a legitimate monarch was based on a sense of hereditary legitimacy within patriarchal estates. Its Catholicism was based on a loyalty to an unbroken lineage of church hierarchy. Its social relations, stretching from top to bottom of a little world which, like an Indian village today, was content to live without secrets and without privacy, was fundamentally a feudal one. Nineteenth-century man suddenly discovered that his passion for the medieval could be fed by a memory of a world that had vanished from one remote region of Britain only two generations before.

The past has survived, then, or survived at least in recollection, if we know where to look and whom to ask. It was the historical novelist who went to look and to ask. If modern man makes free in his mind of more than one age and nation, and moves at will through many worlds not his own, this is among the reasons why he can do so.

9 *Things on the Mind*

What is the place of things – physical objects – in novels?

Novels are about people, and the role of things there is always likely to be a secondary one. And yet many readers like being told about them. The novel informs about something more than human nature: it explains how to deal with a shipwrecked vessel if cast away on a desert island, cook a meal or hunt whales. *Humphry Clinker* explains why the water of Glasgow is too hard, and what could be done about it; *Lolita*, among other matters, about American motels. Fiction can inform about things in a very simple sense.

A novelist can push his emphasis here in either direction, towards things or minds. At the broadest, there are two possibilities: objects may be offered in and for themselves, or purely as evidences of character and outlook. That spectrum has its interesting middle point: Scott perceptively observed of *Humphry Clinker* that it was based on the notion of 'describing the various effects produced upon different members of the same family by the same objects', and the motto to the first volume of *Tristram Shandy*, from Epictetus, reads: 'It is not actions, but opinions concerning actions, that disturb men.'

The liveliest area on this spectrum surely lies towards the middle, whether in fiction or in life. Things in life itself can be symbolic of persons, and we judge individuals by the clothes they wear and the homes they live in, among other considerations. The extremes of the spectrum matter little: one extreme would be to see things only in and for themselves, as in the *chosisme* of Alain Robbe-Grillet – a certain formula for tedium; the other, to see them as totally symbolic, like Miss Havisham's decaying wedding cake and gown in *Great Expectations* – symbols of her refusal to forgive the man who once jilted her on her wedding day. But the most notable instances lie between. Moby Dick is a real whale as well as a symbol of evil, or of any object of man's quixotic courage to dare and to defeat. Since things are often symbolic in life as well as in art, and yet remain themselves, that ambiguity need not be thought of as taxing. It is certainly not unrealistic.

A novel can be drawn in either direction, towards a sense of things or a sense of mind. Outside and inside will always need to be intelligibly related, much as an architect relates the interior of a building to its outer shell. It was an ambition of high Victorian fiction to drive the novel inwards, to mentalise events, and to see all significant action as ultimately an action of mind. Early in the century, Scott had thought of that emphasis as feminine, and it is certainly uncharacteristic of his own novels. There can be 'too much attempt to put the reader exactly up to the thoughts and sentiments of the parties', he complained in his journal (28 March 1826) of a novel he had been reading, adding that 'the women do this better'. The outer view, in this interpretation, is the masculine view: it is the view of Fielding and Scott, of Balzac and Dickens. But that, admittedly, would leave Richardson and Henry James, who glory in mental events, on the feminine side.

The tradition of the 'inner', however feminine in its origins – by women, often enough, or at least for them – has a mixed descent. Kipling remarks in 'The Janeites' that Jane Austen left lawful issue in the shape of a son, his name being Henry James; and the Brontës are more inward than either, reaching far beneath thought to encounter passion and instinct. The tradition of the 'outer' is paradoxically harder to grasp. Since houses and their furnishings comprise the chief things of fiction, one might ask where the first real room in English fiction is: the first one could draw or paint in convincing detail without imaginative additions. The answer may well be the wretched room in a sponging-house in High Holborn where Richardson's Clarissa is miserably confined – an odd fact, if true, since Richardson is among the first great masters of the inner, and it is surprising to claim for him that he saw the outer world more precisely and firmly than Defoe or Fielding. But though Defoe and Fielding plainly prefer the world of outer reality, they do not often make us see it in its minute particulars. Solid objects in *Crusoe* and *Tom Jones* exist in relation to character rather than in themselves, like the tools that Crusoe takes from the wreck, or the muff that Sophia leaves in the inn at Upton to symbolise her indignation at Tom's infidelity.

Richardson does more than that. But then he is writing a modern equivalent of Spenser's *Faerie Queene* and of Bunyan's *Pilgrim's Prog-*

ress; and Spenser, especially, could equip an allegorical idea with a
mighty battery of objects. Consider Mammon's cave:

> Both roof, and floor, and walls were all of gold,
> But overgrown with dust and old decay,
> And hid in darkness, that none could behold
> The hue thereof . . .

> In all that room was nothing to be seen
> But huge great iron chests and coffers strong,
> All barred with double bands. . . . (II, vii, 29–30)

The description is extensive: a vast tableau minutely detailed to make
one see.

The tradition of the 'outer', then, hard as it is to trace, may take its
rise out of ancient epic and Renaissance romance, and work its way
into the English novel through Richardson, Smollett and Scott.
Walter Bagehot, in his essay on Scott (1858), perceptively remarked
how Scott omitted 'the delineation of the soul', and justly praised him
as a novelist in the British empirical tradition: 'Above all minds, his
had the Baconian propensity to work upon "stuff".' But a literary
interest in stuff is a lot older than British empiricism: it runs back to
the long account of the shield of Achilles in the eighteenth *Iliad*. It is
older than any recorded philosophical tradition, and far older than
the novel itself.

★

The chief stuff of fiction is the house or home, with its appurtenances.
Some instances will serve.

[1719] I consulted several things in my situation, which I found
would be proper for me. First, health and fresh water, I just now
mentioned. Secondly, shelter from the heat of the sun. Thirdly,
security from ravenous creatures, whether men or beasts. Fourthly,
a view of the sea. . . .
Before I set up my tent, I drew half a circle before the hollow
place. . . . In this half-circle I pitched two rows of strong stakes. . . .
The entrance into this place I made to be not by a door, but by a
short ladder to go over the top; which ladder, when I was in, I lifted

over after me, and so I was completely fenced in, and fortified. . . . (Defoe, *Robinson Crusoe*)

[1748] A horrid hole of a house, in an alley they call a court; stairs wretchedly narrow, even to the first-floor rooms: and into a den they led me, with broken walls, which had been papered, as I saw by a multitude of tacks, and some torn bits held on by the rusty heads.

The floor was indeed clean, but the ceiling was smoked with variety of figures, and initials of names, that had been the woeful employment of wretches who had no other way to amuse themselves.

A bed at one corner, with coarse curtains tacked up at the feet to the ceiling; because the curtain-rings were broken off; but a coverlid upon it with a cleanish look, though plaguily in tatters, and the corners tied up in tassels, that the rents in it might go no farther.

The windows dark and double-barred. . . . Four old Turkey-worked chairs. . . . An old, tottering, worm-eaten table. . . . The chimney had two half-tiles in it on one side, and one whole one on the other. . . . An old half-barred stove-grate was in the chimney. . . . To finish the shocking description, in a dark nook stood an old broken-bottomed cae couch, without a squab or coverlid, sunk at one corner. . . . (Richardson, *Clarissa* [Belford to Lovelace, 17 July])

[1813] Every disposition of the ground was good; and she looked on the whole scene, the river, the trees scattered on its banks, and the winding of the valley, as far as she could trace it, with delight. As they passed into other rooms, these objects were taking different positions; but from every window there were beauties to be seen. The rooms were lofty and handsome, and their furniture suitable to the fortune of their proprietor; but Elizabeth saw, with admiration of his taste, that it was neither gaudy nor uselessly fine; with less of splendour, and more real elegance, than the furniture of Rosings.

'And of this place,' thought she, 'I might have been mistress!' (Jane Austen, *Pride and Prejudice* ch. 43)

[1835] The house itself, three storeys high without counting the attics, is built of hewn stone and washed with that yellow shade which gives a mean look to nearly every house in Paris. The five windows at the front on each floor have small panes, and their blinds are all drawn up to different levels so that the lines are at sixes and sevens. . . . The ground-floor is well designed for use as a middle-class boarding-house. . . . Nothing could be more depressing than the sight of the sitting-room, with its various chairs upholstered in a haircloth of alternately dull and shiny stripes. . . . The flooring is uneven. Its walls are panelled to elbow-level. . . . (Balzac, *Le père Goriot*)

[1910] 'The wych-elm I remember. Helen spoke of it as a very splendid tree.'

'It is the finest wych-elm in Hertfordshire. Did your sister tell you about the teeth?'

'No.'

'Oh, it might interest you. There are pigs' teeth stuck into the trunk, about four feet from the ground. The country people put them in long ago, and they think that if they chew a piece of the bark, it will cure the toothache. The teeth are almost grown over now, and no one comes to the tree.'

'I should. I love folklore and all festering superstitions.' (E. M. Forster, *Howards End* ch. 8)

[1925] Bond Street fascinated her; Bond Street early in the morning in the season; its flags flying; its shops; no splash; no glitter; one roll of tweed in the shop where her father had bought his suits for fifty years; a few pearls; salmon on an iceblock.

'That is all,' she said, looking at the fishmonger's. 'That is all,' she repeated, pausing for a moment at the window of a glove shop where, before the War, you could buy almost perfect gloves. And her old Uncle William used to say a lady is known by her shoes and her gloves. (Virginia Woolf, *Mrs Dalloway*)

These six extracts span more than two centuries, but their similarities are perhaps more striking than any differences. Not one of these novelists is interested in objects for themselves: not one describes a thing except in its relation to character. Defoe even uses the word 'things' to mean considerations relating to the wellbeing of his hero: health, water, shelter and security. The sponging-house where the divine Clarissa is humiliatingly detained, though marvellously detailed, is still a symbol of her humiliation: the surprising details of the clean floor and coverlid are needed to explain the purity of the figure she makes there, 'the kneeling lady, sunk with majesty too in her white flowing robes' in a corner of that ugly room. And in Jane Austen, Darcy's home at Pemberley, in Derbyshire, means Darcy himself to Elizabeth Bennet, who visits it as a tourist – a reflection of the personality of the admirer whose offer of marriage she has only recently and unjustly rejected. Balzac's shabby old *pension* 'Vauquer', in a run-down quarter of Paris, aspires to some life of its own; but it is life that soon turns into mirror-image of an old man deserted by his daughters. Balzac's originality here lies in his readiness to describe such things to his readers before he has so much as introduced his characters or suggested any symbolic relation with them. That is a highly nineteenth-century technique, even Victorian, as in Dickens's account of foggy London in the opening of *Bleak House*: it would look over-long in eighteenth-century fiction, or now. Jane Austen rarely allows herself more than a sentence or two of description at a time, and interlaces her account of objects with a remark that draws the interest back firmly into the standpoint of a character: 'As they passed into other rooms, these objects were taking different positions', she remarks of the river and the trees, imagining Elizabeth's walk within the windows of Pemberley.

It is always a sense of the symbolic that enriches. Forster sees Mrs Wilcox's beloved country house, 'Howards End', as a symbol of ancestral calm and traditional virtues – so much so that he does not altogether rescue it from the charge of the idyllic, or persuade the reader that it exists as a solid object. By now symbol has usurped solidity; a few pages on, and Mrs Wilcox triumphs unexpectedly over Margaret Schlegel, a cosmopolite of intellectual tastes, with a sudden plea for the solid. When Margaret tells her: 'Discussion keeps a house alive. It cannot stand by bricks and mortar alone', the older woman replies:

> It cannot stand without them, and. . . I sometimes think that it is wiser to leave action and discussion to men. (ch. 9)

It is simply difficult for those of cultured inclinations to see things in and for themselves. And not only for them: educated or not, we all look at things for what they can tell us about ourselves and others.

The strongest role for a thing in fiction is expressive, then, as a signifier of a human quality: like Sophia's muff in *Tom Jones*, or the closet-bed where Lockwood sleeps in *Wuthering Heights*, to dream of Cathy, whose bed it once was: a bed where Heathcliff himself, in unappeased love for her, is fated to die. And when mind and sensibility conquer all, as in Virginia Woolf, things are humanly suggestive or they are nothing. Mrs Dalloway knew no language and no history, we are told, and seldom read a book; and what she sees in shop-windows simply reminds her of what her father did and what her uncle thought.

★

Are novelists, then, ever interested in things as such, or concerned to describe them?

The first step in answering is to consider what a description would look like in the context of narrative. To tell a story is to involve oneself in objects, such as homes and garments apt to the rank and style of the characters who use them. But all that is simply like life, and to say that is simply to confirm that novelists tell of life as people live it. The symbol is the extreme instance of that kind of seeing, but an instance which is itself lifelike. People in life often suit the houses they inhabit, or come to resemble their decorations and their pets.

'Why is the world, which seems so near, so hard to get hold of?' Patrick White once exclaimed. There are two large difficulties. One is that a given language such as English is simply unable to describe all the objects around us. There is a well-known party game designed to induce a certain circular gesture of the hand, and the trick is done by asking what a spiral staircase is. And how, without gesturing, *can* one explain what a spiral staircase is, unless in a language too technical to be acceptable?

The other difficulty is that the novelist cannot reasonably or tolerably describe at length things that every reader knows. Things in novels are not usually like Homer's shield of Achilles. Rooms, garments and domestic objects are part of the shared experience of novelist and reader, and it would be tedious to itemise their attributes. 'Nothing but *fact* could authorize so much particularity', Shenstone once protested in a letter against the prolixity of *Clarissa*, 'and indeed not that' (23 March 1750).

The movement from Defoe towards Virginia Woolf is none the less of a perceptible kind. One aspect of that change concerns story itself. Crusoe builds a stockade in a deliberated order of events: first he considers what he will need of his dwelling place, then he draws a line on the ground, then he drives in stakes . . . By contrast, Mrs Dalloway is *thought* by Bond Street rather than thinking it: the street governs her consciousness, and not she it – but governs it only lightly, since her thoughts fly off into tangents. The time sequence is not lost; a stream of consciousness is still a stream. But the shift from outer to inner, over two centuries, has palpably weakened the momentum of narrative, and has slowed sequence even further in the direction of tableau. Defoe builds towards an event, such as settling into a stockade and pulling the ladder up after: Forster and Virginia Woolf towards a total mood, or something of high abstracted import. 'Life is not a series of gig lamps symmetrically arranged', as she famously re-marked in her essay on 'Modern Fiction' (1919), but

> a luminous halo, a semi-transparent envelope surrounding us from the beginning of consciousness to the end.

Forster's view of fiction is less radically inner than that, and he encases his narratives in a sheath of things which are arranged, if not symmetrically, at least in the orderly pattern of events themselves. Thoughts triumph over things in Forster; but things still need to be there, if only to be triumphed over. 'There are moments', he pro-nounces in *Howards End*, as the Schlegel sisters debate Margaret's impending marriage,

> when the inner life actually 'pays', when years of self-scrutiny, conducted for no ulterior motive, are suddenly of practical use (ch. 23),

adding that

> Such moments are still rare in the West; that they come at all promises a fairer future.

Things matter here when they partake of the life of mind, and move from the dignified status of symbols to the still more dignified standing of breathing and reflecting creatures with a will of their own. 'The house has a surer life than we', Helen observes of Howards End (ch. 37).

Hard as it is for novelists to see things clearly and for themselves, it is just as hard for anyone else. The problem of the novel here is the problem of life. That is why it remains unconvincing to compare the work of the novelist to the natural scientist's – unconvincing about science as well as about novels. In no advanced intellectual activity does one begin by collecting facts and end by interpreting them: that is a purely fictional view of scientific process. Karl Popper tells in his *Conjectures and Refutations* (1963) how he used to ask his class in Vienna: 'Carefully observe, and write down what you have observed' (p. 46) – at which, of course, his students looked utterly baffled, and asked what he wanted them to observe. Observation that is purposeful is always selective, never mere documentation. It notes and describes what is significant.

Zola, unfortunately, was not a member of Popper's class, and his illusion was precisely what Popper was concerned to refute. In *Le Roman expérimental* (1880), half a century earlier, he called the novelist 'equally an observer and an experimentalist', but wrote as if observation necessarily precedes experiment:

> The observer in him gives the facts as he has observed them, suggests the point of departure, displays the solid earth on which his characters are to tread, and the phenomena to develop. Then the experimentalist appears, and introduces an experiment: that is to say, sets his characters going in a certain story so as to show that the succession of facts will be such as the requirements of the determination of the phenomena under examination call for.

But this is an incredible view of what novelists do. A novelist is far more likely to begin with a story than with observed facts, or at least with the central situation in a story – what Henry James in his notes loved to call a 'germ'. Facts matter when story requires them to matter. Crusoe existed in Defoe's mind, one may feel sure, before he thought of the stakes or the ladder.

Henry James often tells in his notebooks how such conception happens, often from a hint in conversation. *The Aspern Papers* was born in his mind in Florence in January 1887, though he was to cover his tracks by changing Florence into Venice, and Byron into an imaginary American poet:

> Hamilton . . . told me a curious thing of Capt Silsbee, the Boston art-critic and Shelley-worshipper; that is, of a curious adventure of

his. Miss Claremont, Byron's ci-devant mistress (the mother of Allegra) was living, here in Florence, at a great age, 80 or thereabouts, and with her lived her niece . . . Silsbee knew they had interesting papers . . .

James calls this 'a little subject', altering the ending ingeniously from an offer of marriage by the niece to an oblique suggestion by the aunt. The things James needed, like the Aspern manuscripts that were eventually burnt, or the fading palazzo where the old ladies lived, are pale existences indeed beside the emotions of the three characters. So are Mrs Gereth's treasures in *The Spoils of Poynton*, which also end in flames. James calls her passion for her things 'almost maniacal', but he is far more interested in her passion than in her things:

> 'Things' were of course the sum of the world; only, for Mrs Gereth, the sum of the world was rare French furniture and Oriental china. She could at a stretch imagine people's not having, but she couldn't imagine their not wanting and not missing. (ch. 3)

But they could be other than French and oriental, and the novel would still be what it is. Readers can be easily satisfied in such matters, and the faintness of most things in fiction explains why they are so easy to offer, since the real offerings are elsewhere. James convinces us that Poynton is indeed a treasure house, and its destruction by fire a catastrophe, without more than the sketchiest of indicative details about what they were:

> When she could really see again, she was on a sofa in the drawing-room, staring with intensity at an object soon distinct as the great Italian cabinet that, at Poynton, had been in the red saloon. Without looking, she was sure the room was occupied with other objects like it. . . . (ch. 7)

As Fleda's gloved hand touches the sofa and thrills to the feel of old brocade, it is her wavering sensations that are worth following, not the china or the sofa. Reality, as Flaubert once remarked in an angry letter to Turgenev (8 November 1877), is 'no more than a springboard', and Zola's articles made his blood boil every Monday, suggesting as they did that 'to it alone belongs the Kingdom!' That is what it was like to invent Naturalism, 'principles that are shrivelling his brain' (14 November 1876). The naturalists, he believed, were humbugs who wanted everyone to think they had discovered the Mediterranean for themselves.

But Flaubert's indignation was too moderate, and the truth is that reality is not even a springboard. The novelist does not begin with real things and end in creation. He begins somewhere else.

★

All this may help to explain how it is possible for a novelist to describe things he has never seen or experienced. There can be no reasonable doubt that this is so. Defoe described Crusoe's stockade, it seems likely, without ever having built one himself, or watched anyone else at that work. Richardson's priggish letter to a lady denying he had ever in his life been to a ball or to a house of ill repute is altogether likely to be true. The least convincing of Forster's novels, *Maurice* (1971), describes a relationship dear to his heart, and a lady who never saw a battlefield has described one in the Western desert, and in these sufficient terms:

> The enemy seemed to be on the alert. Repeated gun flashes dotted the German positions and the men, who were in close order, instinctively kept closer than need be as they marched into no-man's-land. The moon had set and they moved by starlight. There was little to see, and Simon thought it unlikely that anyone had seen them, yet, a few hundred yards from their objective, a flare went up from the hill-top, blanching the desert and revealing the two close-knit platoons. Immediately there was uproar. Red and yellow tracer bullets, like deadly fireworks, passed overhead and machine-guns kept up their mad, virulent rattle. Simon shouted 'Run for it'.... (Olivia Manning, *The Danger Tree* [1977] ch. 7)

It is tempting to guess how the elements divide here: the details that were supplied on request, like the colour of tracer bullets; those that any intelligent being knows, or could guess, like the gun flashes; and those supplied by a sense of drama, like the men who kept in closer order than they were commanded to do. The one certain thing is that nobody needed to be there in order to write about it.

It is not even certain that having been there would have helped. Stephen Crane had never seen a battle when he wrote *The Red Badge of*

Courage (1895), and became a war correspondent only afterwards. William Golding once cheerfully remarked of *The Spire* (1964), a novel about medieval architecture and sexual frustration, that he knew as much about the one as about the other. No wonder if the Zola-fad was quick-passing in Western fiction: few novelists now cock their notebooks to record the right phrase for the sought-out object or the contrived moment, or suppose that observation must precede description. Flaubert's counterblast about reality as only a springboard, fierce as it sounds, was not fierce enough.

★

How, then, do novelists know about the things they describe?

The answer, which is not meant to be deflating, is that often enough they do not: or not, at least, in any exceptional sense. Their task is to appear to know. Since art is more than life, and needs to be, that answer measures the true dignity of fiction: living, after all, is what everybody does. 'The less you feel a thing', Flaubert once wrote to a correspondent, 'the fitter you are to express it as it is' (6 July 1852), though he added that 'you must be able to make yourself feel it'. Conrad's experience of the sea has been shared by thousands who never took to literature or proved a Conrad. What he knew about the East, where he spent only a few weeks ashore, could easily be excelled by thousands of nineteenth-century Europeans, and by many more since. Somerset Maugham, propped at the bar of a Singapore hotel and listening to the stories of Malay planters, or Henry James absorbing the anecdotes he called germs at London and Paris dinner-parties – these are the supreme images of the novelist on the prowl for material. Borges once remarked that real things can be a nuisance: 'If you're a materialist, if you believe in hard and fast things, then you're tied down by reality, or by what you call reality.'[1] Things, in his view, need to be 'dissolved' by thought to be useable. To see, or to be told, is not enough, and may even impede.

The grand exception is childhood and youth, which no novelist needs to fabricate, since everyone has known it. To recreate the mind of a child, and to see things as a child sees them, is a belated discovery in fiction, and one that hardly existed at all before the nineteenth century. But there is no denying that *David Copperfield*, *Kim* and *Le Grand Meaulnes*, like Proust's great novel, are works of experiential power, and that no reader could bear to be told that their creators had not in some measure lived them and edited them by the processes of memory. But then childhood is something that nobody chooses. The Indian landscapes in *Kim*, or the *madeleine* that starts a long chain of recollection in Proust, are things not sought after by the artist, being drawn up from a deeper life than he could ever choose to live.

NOTES

1. Richard Burgin, *Conversations with Jorge Luis Borges* (New York, 1969) p. 158.

10 *Scene-making*

Sometimes, in a public spot, a face can recall the style of a great painter, and one reflects how it might have interested Botticelli or Rembrandt. The reader of novels can find this happens in life: he can witness, or take part in, a scene that suddenly recalls a novelist he knows.

A few novelists – a very few – have even given their names to the language as epithets, as 'Dickensian' can mean a living version of superabundant jollity, like Dingley Dell in *Pickwick*, or alternatively an animated slum; or as an experience can be *proustien* when a nostalgic recollection is triggered by a taste or smell; or Kafkaesque if born of a nameless horror of a bureaucratic machine. Scenes can hardly be Trollopian, but characters can, especially if they are portly clergymen. But these instances, it may be significant, are based only on a seemingly superficial acquaintance with a novelist, and usually with his earlier works.

The problem of the novelist's hallmark is at once compelling and fugitive, and multiple in its aspects. How does one recognise a novelist's characteristic atmospheric strength? How do scenes that embody such strengths relate to the whole work? And how, over the centuries, has the range of available themes widened the subject-matter of fiction? To discuss such questions at all is to risk confusing them, since they are intimately interrelated. But to omit them, tempting as it is, is too easy. The permissible matter of fiction today is vastly wider than it was in the decades around 1700, and one way to consider that growth is to study how scenes have been handled by great novelists, and what they have put into them. The attempt is bound to be tentative, and probably untidy.

A catalogue of themes can do no more, certainly, than open the question out to view. Some themes in fiction are personal; others verge upon the national, as the house-party novel between Peacock and P. G. Wodehouse is characteristic of England among all the nations, or as the novel of ideas of German fiction between Goethe and Thomas Mann. The range of subjects and settings can widen, even narrow, over the centuries, and from nation to nation. So can the compelling details and sense of pace that animates them.

★

A novelist, like any professional, needs to know his own strength. Thackeray was once congratulated on that richly ambiguous moment in *Vanity Fair* where Becky, at the instant when she faces ruin, suddenly respects her husband for striking down her lover before her eyes. 'When I wrote that sentence', Thackeray exclaimed appreciatively, 'I slapped my fist on the table, and said: that is a touch of genius.'¹ It would be interesting to make a mental anthology of such moments where strength suddenly shows. There is an astounding detail near the end of *Sons and Lovers* where D. H. Lawrence has his hero's sister giggle as she stirs poison into the warm milk by which, lovingly, they plan to kill a suffering mother; or that strange instant, unimaginable in its cold ferocity in any fiction earlier than this century, where a wife in Ford's *The Good Soldier* finds her husband's mistress dead of a heart-attack in her hotel room:

> Maisie had died in the effort to strap up a great portmanteau. She had died so grotesquely that her little body had fallen forward into the trunk, and it had closed upon her, like the jaws of a gigantic alligator. . . . She was smiling, as if she had just scored a goal in a hockey match. (I, vi)

Henry James noticed the abiding interest of the question, and saw, too, how ultimately unanswerable it was. Every great novelist, he suggested in 'The Lesson of Balzac' (1905), has his own landscape – a pageant of scenes, or scenery – which is unique to himself, since no other such landscape can 'receive the solar rays at the same angle':

> Why is it that the life that overflows in Dickens seems to me always to go on in the morning, or in the very earliest hours of the afternoon at most, and in a vast apartment that appears to have windows, large, uncurtained and rather unwashed windows, on all sides at once? Why is it that in George Eliot the sun sinks forever in the

west, and the shadows are long, and the afternoon wanes, and the trees vaguely rustle, and the colour of the day is much inclined to yellow? Why is it that in Charlotte Brontë we move through an endless autumn? Why is it that in Jane Austen we sit quite resigned in an arrested spring . . . ?

All that suggests an area for debate, if nothing more. A novelist possesses his own landscape, which is his, presumably, by virtue of the manner in which he governs the pace and matter of his story.

★

The point about pace can be most clearly made by a contrast with one of the chief ancestors of modern fiction, the long prose romance of the Renaissance and after. Works like Sidney's *Arcadia* (1590–3) are composed in a ponderous alternation of story and set speech: a technique of enormous sententious weight, but hardly adapted to making a dramatic moment tell. In a number of seventeenth-century novels, and later in Lesage and Defoe, it has been abandoned in favour of a brisker interplay between speech and event. That interplay is often comic, and most notably picaresque. It can be less than brisk in memoir-novels, and absent from early letter-novels, where a tradition of classical rhetoric and romance narrative lives on: the *Lettres portugaises* are extended exercises in sentiment, above all the sentiment of pathos; and Richardson's most imposing scenes are sustained in a way that could make even his contemporaries impatient.

Defoe, Lesage, Fielding, Sterne, Smollett – all point an episode like an anecdote, whether comic or serious; and their novels accumulate such anecdotes, tidily or untidily, into long chains. Defoe often seems content to end his chain in arbitrary fashion: at the end of the first part of *Crusoe* he leaves himself free to continue the story into a second part if he chooses, as in the event he did. Fielding imposes an order – conscious, evidently, that the novel needs to acquire the dignity of symmetrical form; though the texture of much of the narrative within these limits is not radically different from Lesage's or Defoe's. And the tradition of linked anecdotes lingers on into the Victorian age, with much in *Pickwick*, *Oliver Twist* and *Nicholas Nickleby* that smacks of it: indeed, Dickens is capable of reverting to that manner of writing as late as the 1860s, as in *Our Mutual Friend*. It is not, however, favoured by the two great Regency novelists, Jane Austen and Scott; and it is not upheld by novelists who arrived as late as the 1850s, such as Trollope, George Eliot and Meredith.

There are arguments to be made on both sides. The long, sustained passages of Richardson undeniably allow a scene to be 'made', if the reader is patient enough. The episodic tradition from Defoe to Dickens, by contrast, allows to a scene the quick point of a dagger-thrust; if it fails, little enough is lost, and the author can try again. That is what makes Richardson's *grands tableaux*, like the deathbed of Clarissa, so difficult to compare with a scene by Defoe or Fielding. After 1800 much of fiction moved away from these early models towards a texture at once more consistent and more flexible than either of them. Jane Austen never allows her characters long speeches, as Scott occasionally does; but neither is she episodic.

As the inhibition against the easy introduction of dialogue into narrative fades during the nineteenth century, one impediment to a consistency of texture is progressively removed, and events can move effortlessly into direct speech, and out again. Technique grows suppler, and richer in nuance. 'Free indirect speech', which is uncommon in eighteenth-century novels, is one evidence of that advance.

But the movement is not always towards economy. Though few novelists after 1800 would attempt to sustain a single note for as long as Richardson sustains the dying of Clarissa, none would consume so much story, and so swiftly, as Defoe does in *Crusoe*, or Smollett in *Peregrine Pickle*. Today the novel is neither as slow as the one nor as fast as the other. It has found its own speed: one brisk enough for maintaining interest, but deliberate enough to create effects that are memorably many-sided.

★

The matter of fiction grows wider, for good or ill. It might be rewarding to consider how topics enter the permissible realm of fiction, which by the late Victorian age embraces most matters of intelligent discourse outside the more technical aspects of the sciences. All suggestions are tentative here, however, and await further evidence.

CHILDREN

These are not fictions written for children, or those where they merely figure, but fictions suggestive of a distinct childish consciousness.

There is an outburst of literary interest in this matter in the late eighteenth century, though much of it is edifying rather than realistic. There are children in *La Nouvelle Héloïse,* where Rousseau even tries to convey an immature consciousness through letters composed by a child. Campe's *Robinson der jüngere* appeared in 1779–80, a German's childhood sequel to *Crusoe*; and Thomas Day's *Sandford and Merton* (1783) is an enlightened model of childish virtue, though some would say it suggests little observation of real children.

The mind of a child, with its characteristic vulnerability, enters fiction more decisively with Maria Edgeworth's *Harrington* (1817), which begins with child trauma. A small boy is threatened by his nurse at bedtime with the cry of a Jewish pedlar outside in the street; he grows up an anti-semite, and then falls in love, as he believes, with a Jewish lady. (The novel may be the first fictional study of racial prejudice as well.) That hint is developed by Dickens twenty years later, in *Oliver Twist,* and in the early chapters of *David Copperfield,* which echoes *Jane Eyre* (1847) three years earlier, both showing a child reading a book and responding childishly; and Lewis Carroll's Alice stories appeared soon after, in 1865–72. The topic is powerfully Victorian, though with late eighteenth-century pioneers, and still more twentieth-century: Proust's *Du côté de chez Swann* (1913), Richard Hughes's *High Wind in Jamaica* (1929), Dorothy Bussy's *Olivia, by Olivia* (1949), and L. P. Hartley's *Go-between* (1953).

HOMOSEXUALS

Two novels of 1748, both English, attempt the subject in brief episodes. Smollett's *Roderick Random* has a homosexual nobleman, Earl Strutwell, who tries to seduce a sexually innocent though fortune-hunting hero; and in John Cleland's *Fanny Hill* the heroine observes two youths in an inn through a hole in the wall. Both are presented indignantly, though in Cleland the indignation is the thinnest of disguises for a lyrically pornographical interest; the episode was cut from the first French version in 1751, and translated for the first time in 1771. The matter is mentioned as a covert accusation against the Jesuits by Voltaire in *Candide* (1759), and is a major theme in Diderot's *La Religieuse,* written a dozen years after *Random* but published only posthumously, in 1796; and it is hinted at, but not developed, in Laclos's *Les Liaisons dangereuses* in 1782.

Hinting apart, the theme is rare in nineteenth- and early twentieth-century fiction, at least in novels offered openly and lawfully for sale.

A homosexual first chapter for Lawrence's *Women in Love* (1920) was omitted from published editions, though it has since appeared in a journal (*Texas Quarterly* [1963]); Lawrence had already touched on the subject in *The Rainbow* (1915), which treats an incipiently lesbian affair between Ursula Brangwen and Winifred Inger. But it has emerged powerfully only since the 1950s, with Christopher Isherwood's *World in the Evening* (1954) and James Baldwin's *Giovanni's Room* (1957), both sympathetic to the point of sentimentality.

PERFORMANCES

The adventures of strolling players is a subject for fiction at least as early as Scarron's *Roman comique* (1651-7), and often echoed, as in Dickens's *Nicholas Nickleby* (1839), where the 'starved business' of acting is presented less in its loose morals than in a manner affectionately picaresque. Attendance by a character in the audience has a more interesting history. It can be a point in a young man's round of experience and a part of growing up, like Gil Blas's visit to a theatre in Granada, or Tom Jones's to one in London (XVI, v) to see Garrick play Hamlet – an occasion, mainly, for Partridge's imbecile comments on the acting; and Rousseau, who introduces an Italian singer into a private house in *La Nouvelle Héloïse* (1761), later sends his hero to the Paris opera (book 2).

There is a higher interest, largely nineteenth-century and since, in performances expressive of the character and mood of those who listen and watch, as in Emma's visit to the opera in Flaubert's *Madame Bovary* (1857) to hear *Lucia di Lammermoor*. Charlotte Brontë's figure of the actress Rachel in *Villette* (1853) is as profoundly revelatory of the author herself as of her heroine: she had seen Rachel in London two years before, and felt the performance had 'revealed a glimpse of hell' to her. Such glimpses can occur in that century at evening parties as well as in theatres – favourite grounds in that age for an assertion of social status and the search for a match. The piano recital in George Eliot's last novel, *Daniel Deronda* (1876), is perhaps the richest instance: Gwendolen Harcleth, the heroine, is jealous of another young lady who plays the piano better; but the scene is dominated by Julius Klesmer, a master pianist whose performance recalls happy days more than twenty years before, in Weimar, with Liszt.

By the mid-century the performer in English fiction is often felt as an exciting alien. Klesmer is less likely to be a recollection of Liszt himself than of one Anton Rubinstein, whom George Eliot also met in

Weimar in 1854, 'a felicitous combination of the German, the Sclave, and the Semite', as the novel calls him; the musician Emilia in Meredith's *Sandra Belloni* (1864) is half-Italian; the actress in Henry James's *Tragic Muse* (1890) is Franco-American; and the fat, ugly soprano heard in a Tuscan opera in Forster's *Where Angels Fear to Tread* (1905) is based on a memory of Tetrazzini, whom Forster as a young man had heard sing in Florence. All this is a world, or at any rate an English Channel, away from the amateur theatricals planned and interrupted in Jane Austen's *Mansfield Park* (1814), or the English village musicians in Hardy's *Under the Greenwood Tree* (1872). It is partly a reflection of an English sense of inferiority, in that half century and more, to the continental achievement in the performing arts – an inferiority that no longer has cause to be felt. But it is wider than that: a sense of a moral incompleteness in English social inhibition that an alien performer of genius can perturb or shatter, even in the polite arena of the drawing-room. Music and play are great disturbers in these novels: as the characters in the fifth chapter of Forster's *Howards End* (1910) listen to Beethoven's Fifth Symphony, they reveal in their private thoughts more of their emotional lives than they would readily do in talk; and Margaret Schlegel's superiority over the rest lies in the fact that she does not imagine things, like her sister, but 'can only see the music'.

WORKS OF ART

These are rarely integral to plot, though artists can be: perhaps Oscar Wilde's *Portrait of Dorian Gray* (1891) is among the few instances in a novel where a work of art functions indispensably within the story, almost as if it were itself a character, as the picture of a depraved youth takes on the evidences of his depravity.

This, too, is a nineteenth-century element in fiction, though seldom a thriving one. Stendhal and Balzac were both connoisseurs of Italian art, and scenes in *Le Rouge et le noir* (1830) may owe details to paintings by Guercino and Luini. Peacock's *Headlong Hall* includes a walk through a landscape garden, with an exchange between the characters on the principle of 'unexpectedness' in art which is itself a contribution to the debate on the picturesque, though more a witty than a substantial one:

'Pray, sir,' said Mr Milestone, 'by what name do you distinguish this character, when a person walks round the ground for the second time?' (ch. 4)

Hawthorne introduces a statue into the opening of *The Marble Faun* (1860), an idea Norman Douglas may have borrowed in *South Wind* (1917); the hero of Balzac's *La Cousine Bette* (1846) is a Polish sculptor; Mr Bounderby's portrait looks down upon him unchangingly, in the last paragraphs of *Hard Times* (1854), as he ages beneath it. In this century, moreover, there have been numerous novels about the lives of artists, such as Somerset Maugham's *Moon and Sixpence* (1919) and Joyce Cary's *Horse's Mouth* (1944); but these are novels about artists and their supposed love of bohemian life, hardly about works of art. The highest significance accorded to the work itself in fiction is as symbol of character, like the Bronzino portrait that Milly Theale is taken to see in James's *Wings of the Dove* (1902), because it looks like her. Milly herself becomes a Renaissance princess by that comparison, or something still more heroic, though she acutely glimpses her own early fate in the portrait, since the lady (as she puts it) is 'dead, dead, dead'.

POLITICS

It is highly debateable what constitutes the first political novel in Europe. If politics means public life along with the moral and personal choices that men make in that life, then novels like Smollett's *Roderick Random* (1748) may reasonably be excluded. A young hero looking for a patron is barely a start here, and mere advancement (or the hope of it) is not enough: one rightly demands an element of ideas and a sense of principle. Maria Edgeworth's *Patronage* (1814) is indeed about principle, but high principle there seems to demand one should stay out of public life for fear of its temptations.

Stendhal's *Le Rouge et le noir* (1830), about a young man's divided ambition between state and church; comes much closer. It even presents a conflict of ideas, between a young Bonapartist hero and his legitimist employer in the days of the restored French monarchy that followed Waterloo; but the interest moves sharply away from politics towards love as the novel progresses. For reasons altogether different, Dickens misses the title of a political novelist, in spite of his passionate interest in public causes: *Bleak House* (1853), which has as strong a title as any of his, is about legal and administrative reform; and in a parliamentary state like Victorian Britain, it is natural to demand an interest in Westminster. And in spite of, or perhaps because of, his early life as a parliamentary reporter, Dickens was never noted for that.

The palm must ultimately go to Disraeli's Coningsby trilogy

(1844–7), written by a young Conservative Member of Parliament, as the works where the continuous life of political fiction truly begins. That life runs on through the industrial novels of the late 1840s and after, such as Elizabeth Gaskell's *Mary Barton* (1848) and Charlotte Brontë's *Shirley* (1849): none of them novels about political parties, but clearly written with a view to influencing public and parliamentary opinion about the new industrial towns of the North. Trollope's six Palliser novels (1864–80) represent the flowering of that tradition, and one of them, *The Prime Minister* (1876), could well claim to be the greatest of all political novels. It appeared in the same year as Meredith's contribution to the species, *Beauchamp's Career.* The 1860s and 1870s are the heyday of that fiction, and above all the years when Gladstone and Disraeli faced each other dramatically across the chamber as leaders of rival parties. Disraeli died in 1881, and the rest of the century shows a weakening interest, though James attempted an uncongenial theme concerning anarchists in *The Princess Casamassima* (1886); and a young Member of Parliament is presented, not altogether convincingly, in *The Tragic Muse* (1890). Twentieth-century interest is discontinuous, and not always parliamentary. Joyce Cary, as a Liberal, wrote his second trilogy, beginning with *Prisoner of Grace* (1952), on Westminster life down to the 1920s, with a hero reminiscent of Lloyd George; but C. P. Snow's novels have represented Whitehall rather than Westminster.

The political novel is a comment on politics rather than a political act. Winston Churchill once wrote a novel in the manner of Disraeli, *Savrola* (1900), but he did not attempt fiction again after entering the Commons in that year. If we except that instance as a sport, then Disraeli remains the only British novelist to become a prime minister, and the only prime minister who was a novelist.

The form is now international, and American novels on Congress and the presidency have abounded since the 1960s: a lonely pioneer being Henry Adams's *Democracy* (1879), a novel of Washington life by the grandson and great-grandson of a president. French, German and Italian fiction includes novels about public and social issues, such as Zola's and Musil's. But the political novel of sustained and exemplary interest remains the Westminster novel between Disraeli and Trollope.

UNIVERSITIES

Few of the great English novelists studied at a British university before the present century. Sterne and Thackeray, who were both at Cambridge, are exceptions, and Fielding studied abroad at Leyden. No woman qualified to enter, though they might hear of such matters, as Jane Austen implies in *Northanger Abbey*. Nothing amounts to an eighteenth-century university novel in English, unless Francis Coventry's *Pompey the Little* (1751), an entertaining affair about Cambridge written by a Fellow of Magdalene.

By the nineteenth century, however, it is common for a hero to pass through a university, if only to acquire some amorous experience and a pile of debts. *Reginald Dalton* (1823), by John Gibson Lockhart, Scott's son-in-law, has some claim to be considered the first university novel, being mainly set in Oxford; in Thackeray's *Pendennis* (1849–50) and Charles Kingsley's *Alton Locke* (1850), by contrast, the hero pauses in Cambridge in flight for something better, or at least other. Forster's *Longest Journey* (1907) begins in the same place, but quickly gets out of it. So does the hero of Evelyn Waugh's first novel, *Decline and Fall* (1928), except that the place there is Oxford, to return only in the last chapter.

The university novel in its most active life is a creation of the 1950s, starting with C. P. Snow's *The Masters* in 1951, set in a Cambridge college, and followed two years later by Kingsley Amis's *Lucky Jim*, set in a small civic university. The American campus novel was simultaneous, with Mary McCarthy's *Groves of Academe* in 1952. No age has favoured this theme as powerfully as the 1950s and 1960s, and no tradition of fiction so much as the Anglo-American: a fact more revealing about the suddenly expanded scale and status of universities in the English-speaking world than about the state of fiction.

★

Such are some of the varieties of pace and subject-matter that have become available to novelists since the eighteenth century. How, with so much to hand, does the novelist contrive to make a scene that looks totally expressive of his genius?

Thackeray was surely right to bang his fist on the desk when he achieved his moment of triumph in *Vanity Fair*. The moment occurs in the fifty-third chapter, and it expresses that fine-balanced ambiguity, or equivocation, that is the mark of his gift. The best of Thackeray can be read in a double sense: he was a snob who despised snobbery; an intellectual republican, at least in some moods, fascinated by public ceremonies and titles; and a gentleman who wrote for money. Dickens's characteristic clarity of vision would not have suited him: his novels are stable in their significance in a way Thackeray's are not. Is Becky Sharp in *Vanity Fair* the most vital force in the novel, or a scheming harlot against whom virtuous families should learn to shut their gates? The moment that caused Thackeray to bang his fist concentrates that ambiguity at its highest point of intensity: it is a moment that presents his double view in full dramatic, even melodramatic force. A woman as vital as Rebecca wants to know she has married a man and not a puppet, even when his virility unmasks her.

> ... Rawdon Crawley, springing out, seized him by the neckcloth, until Steyne, almost strangled, writhed and bent under his arm. 'You lie, you dog!' said Rawdon. 'You lie, you coward and villain!' And he struck the peer twice over the face with his open hand, and flung him bleeding to the ground. It was all done before Rebecca could interpose. She stood there trembling before him. She admired her husband, strong, brave and victorious.
> 'Come here,' he said. She came up at once.
> 'Take off those things.' She began, trembling, pulling the jewels from her arms, and the rings from her shaking fingers, and held them all in a heap, quivering and looking at him. 'Throw them down,' he said, and she dropped them. He tore the diamond ornament out of her breast, and flung it at Lord Steyne. It cut him on his bald forehead. Steyne wore the scar to his dying day.

A moment later Crawley takes his wife's keys, opens her desk and discovers Lord Steyne's note for a thousand pounds.

The limits to be placed upon Thackeray's technique here are clearer today than they would have looked in 1848. The dialogue is of the briefest and rawest: 'I am innocent', says Becky simply, if falsely, when her husband discovers the note she has locked away. All the narrative indicators are summary. When Becky decides that she admires her husband, we are told simply that and nothing but that. Henry James might have condescendingly muttered something here about 'the infancy of art', as he once did on rereading the Waverley novels. Thackeray is not interested in nuance or suggestion, only in the bold strokes of a scene that evolves too quickly for the actors themselves to ponder at leisure. The events themselves are melodramatic; the inward reflection that accompanies them barely sketched in. A moment before, when Crawley breaks in unexpectedly, Lord Steyne is bending over the sofa to kiss Becky's hand; she starts up 'with a faint scream' on seeing Crawley's white face, and tries 'a smile, a horrid smile, as if to welcome her husband', while her lover grinds his teeth 'with fury in his looks'. The scene is triumphantly stagey. And when Becky is left alone, Thackeray hardly attempts to convey her mind, as if confident that the scene itself has given the reader chances enough to guess it for himself:

> What were her thoughts when he left her? She remained for hours after he was gone, the sunshine pouring into the room, and Rebecca sitting alone on the bed's edge. . . . She knew he would never come back. He was gone for ever. Would he kill himself? she thought – not until after he had met Lord Steyne. She thought of her long past life. . . . What *had* happened? Was she guilty or not? She said not. . . . (ch. 53)

All this marches down the long road that leads towards Joyce and Proust. But, as seen from the 1840s, it looks like a long road indeed: thoughts summarised, and moods compressed, into words that make no attempt to sound like a character's own, and remain unashamedly those of their creator.

If a great scene is one where the novelist fulfils himself, then it need not always represent the most memorable moments in his fiction. It is possible to be struck by an unforgettable effect without feeling it to represent the true character of a novelist, and perhaps (for just that reason) to wish it away. No reader of *Mansfield Park* can doubt the power of that moment, in the last chapter but one, when Edmund damns the light-spoken Mary Crawford as 'spoilt, spoilt', as if he were the voice of some avenging doom. But it is not the nature of Jane Austen's talent, at its best, to express itself so explicitly, to indulge in moral underlining, or to explain what the reader is capable of explaining for himself. This is to unmake a scene. It cannot hold a candle to the moment in *Emma* where the rash heroine cheeks Miss Bates at a picnic and is instantly made to feel her shame, even before she has been told to feel it. To know a novelist is to know what he does best and worst; it is to hope he can stay on course. No reader of any sense wants more disquisitions on historical truth from Tolstoy in *War and Peace*, and he may reasonably regret those that are there. In that regard novelist and reader behave like collaborators, though sometimes quarrelsome ones. They both have the interest of the novel at heart.

★

The landscape of fiction moves from outer to inner, and back again: from events that are visible and audible, to mental events or inner reflection, and back to the visible and the audible. Jane Austen, Dickens and Thackeray stand near the point where fiction is turning inwards, but still hesitates to plunge. That slow plunge lasts from the 1850s, with Flaubert and George Eliot, down to the 1920s, when the movement is reversed and action revives. Many novels since the 1930s, in this regard, are more like Fielding or Jane Austen than they are like Flaubert, George Eliot, or their successors in the stream of consciousness. The novel, after more than half a century of ever more inward reflection, has turned brisk again.

It has also grown diverse in its sense of time and place. A sense of past time grows fashionable with Scott, and of unfamiliar place with Rousseau, Edgeworth, Scott and the Brontës. To make a scene, henceforth, often means to define a place and time in a manner largely unknown to eighteenth-century novelists, and to see character as representative of time and place. The portrait of the old Tory peer Lord Monmouth, in Disraeli's *Coningsby*, perfectly illustrates both, and it could not have been written without the precedent of the Waverley novels. The time is only a dozen years previous to the book, in the Reform Bill agitation of 1831–2, the place the London of high political life; and a frightened schoolboy is about to meet a formidable grandfather he has never seen:

> Coningsby with an uncertain step followed his guide through a bed-chamber, the sumptuousness of which he could not notice, into the dressing-room of Lord Monmouth. . . . The lord of the house slowly rose, for he was suffering slightly from the gout, and his left hand rested on an ivory stick. Lord Monmouth was in height about the middle size, but somewhat portly and corpulent. His countenance was strongly marked; sagacity on the brow, sensuality in the mouth and jaw. . . . But his general mien was truly grand; full of a natural nobility, of which no one was more sensible. Lord Monmouth was not in dishabille; on the contrary, his costume was exact, and even careful. . . . He made Coningsby such a bow as

Louis Quatorze might have bestowed on the ambassador of the United Provinces. Then extending his right hand, which the boy tremblingly touched, Lord Monmouth said:

'How do you like Eton?' (I. 3)

Terrified at the spectacle of this 'superb and icy being', the child bursts into tears.

A scene that depends on a sense of time and place, like this one, can build its total effect only slowly, and then only to an informed readership. A dozen years after the first Reform Act, when *Coningsby* appeared, Englishmen were staring into the prospect of a democratic future with mingled hope and trepidation, and a party leader who is at once noble, like Monmouth, and terribly conscious of his nobility, and who yet hoped to lead his party into an electoral victory, was one of intriguing complexity. It is helpful to recall, what is more, that Louis XIV had tried to conquer the Low Countries, so that Monmouth's bow is frightening as well as elegant. Such are the fruits of placing imaginary characters in historical settings, and of seeing even the present or near-present as an historical period.

Some of these fruits have been abandoned by fiction in the present century, which in observation prefers a more neutral tone. Novelists of high literary ambition now delight less often in the trappings of period. The landscape of modern fiction has commonly ceased to be sumptuous: it is more often a sparse and emptied world, and the novelist himself is less often an awestruck and enthusiastic guide, like Scott or Thackeray, than a fastidious and half-bewildered observer of events which he hardly claims to understand himself. Details of time and place can be all but invisible. In the long and exquisitely shaped opening to Richard Hughes's *Fox in the Attic* (1961), for example, we are not told for several paragraphs who the characters are or why they are there: a delay of a scale inconceivable before the present century:

The younger man was springy and tall and well-built, and carried over his shoulder the body of a dead child. Her thin muddy legs dangled against his chest, her head and arms hung down his back; and at his heels walked a black dog – disciplined, saturated and eager. . . . There was no personal grief in the young man's face but it was awe-struck. . . .

The scene takes longer to build, and withholds its point for a greater period, than would once have been thought tolerable. The style represents a sort of art-prose, as if the novel had tired, for the moment, of its more explicit traditions. It is only secondarily concerned, by now, with telling a story.

A pity, those who love stories are bound to think. No texture, however savourable, can long compensate for that loss. The reader is no longer asked to laugh, or to cry, or to await what happens next. If that is what he wants – and there are millions who still do – he must now descend to the thriller, or return to the novels of another age.

NOTE

1. James Hannay, *A Brief Memoir of the Late Mr Thackeray* (Edinburgh: 1864) pp. 20–1.

11 *How Novelists Write*

How do novelists write: at what time of life, at what hours of the day, and with how much forethought and revision? And what are the surviving evidences from the hands of novelists themselves?

THE TIME OF LIFE

Few of the more notable male novelists of the eighteenth century wrote novels in their youth. Smollett is an exception: *Roderick Random* appeared as his first novel in 1748, when he was twenty-seven; another is Crébillon *fils*, who like Fielding was born in 1707, and who was publishing fiction in his mid-twenties; and Goethe wrote *Werther* (1774) in his twenty-fifth year, though by then already a dramatist.

By and large, however, early fiction is not a youthful activity. Defoe was probably nearly sixty when *Crusoe* appeared in 1719, Richardson fifty-one with *Pamela* (1740), and Fielding in his mid-thirties, and a prolific dramatist, with *Joseph Andrews* (1742). Sterne, likewise, was nearly fifty when the first volume of *Tristram Shandy* appeared in 1760, a provincial clergyman and journalist. And Defoe and Fielding had made their names as men of letters before they attempted novels at all.

It is much the same for Frenchmen. Lesage began as a translator and dramatist, *Le Diable boiteux* only appearing in 1707, when he was thirty-nine; *La Nouvelle Héloïse* when Rousseau was the same age; Voltaire was sixty-five with *Candide* (1759), his first tale having appeared only a dozen years before; and Laclos was forty-one at the publication of *Les Liaisons dangereuses* in 1782. On the other hand, Marivaux was only twenty-four when in 1712 he offered a printer two unfinished novels, though his two major fictions did not appear until he was in his forties; and Prévost was thirty-one when the *Homme de qualité* began to appear in 1728: both borderline cases.

Women may be presumed to have had less to lose than men in reputation, to the extent that they were more often amateurs, and their anonymity better protected. But it is an implication of these facts that a young man in the eighteenth century rarely looked first to novels as a way of making name or fortune in the literary world. That pattern continues into the nineteenth century, though not for long. Scott, an established poet, finished his first novel after long hesitation in his early forties, in 1814; Peacock produced *Headlong Hall* two years after *Waverley*, in 1816, at thirty-one; and Stendhal, a survivor of the eighteenth century in spirit as well as in fact, was forty-seven when *Le Rouge et le noir* appeared in 1830.

By that date, however, the pattern of middle-aged beginners was crumbling fast. Balzac had written plays and hack novels as a young man before *Les Chouans* (1829) made his reputation as a serious novelist at the age of thirty; and *Pickwick* (1836–7) made Dickens famous at twenty-four. From the 1830s onwards, with royalty agreements rather than payment by a flat fee growing commoner, novel writing is a common habit for a young man with a literary bent in search of fame or money or both, though he might have to wait for them. Trollope had to wait till he was forty, with *The Warden* (1855). Many Victorians start early as novelists, whether men or women. The profession was shaking off its reputation for the dubious, whether financial or moral; it was the quickest way to a fortune through pen and ink.

By the twentieth century the original situation is reversed, and the novel draws young talents to itself that are plainly non-fictional, to fail there and succeed elsewhere. George Orwell and Cyril Connolly, it is now plain, were above all critics and polemicists, as Philip Larkin is essentially a poet. That they should have started as novelists at all can only have been an act of homage to the status of fiction in this century, if an essential misreading of their own gifts.

THE TIME OF DAY

Few novelists have left accounts of their own manner of work, at least before it became common to give interviews to journalists, and almost none before the nineteenth century. A novel has the enviable distinction of being capable of being composed in a variety of situations – on holiday, for example, or in bed; Virginia Woolf is said to have written at times standing at a writing desk, as Hemingway always did; and Trollope in his *Autobiography* (1883) tells how he wrote *Barchester Towers* (1857) in a train, and in pencil, his wife copying it out afterwards (ch. 6). But it still seems natural to assume that most novels were written sitting in a room at home. Not always alone, however: Maria Edgeworth, who has left what may be the earliest detailed account of the matter, often wrote in a room full of children. In a long letter of 6 September 1834, on her 'habits of composition', she has described her forty years of authorship: how she kept no commonplace book, only a few little notebooks for facts and references, in spite of her father's urging; and how she had a reasonably good memory, often working without even an outline and inventing everything as she went, so that *Castle Rackrent* (1800) was written without 'plan, sketch or framework'. Her only notable predecessor may be Rousseau, who in his *Confessions* (II, ix) describes how he planned and wrote *La Nouvelle Héloïse*.

The topic, though intriguing, is much neglected. Novel writing is a business, after all, and sometimes a highly profitable one: it might repay work-study. Nobody seems to have considered the question in a general light before Harriet Martineau, who was fond of asking friends who were authors about their manner of work, and who discusses their answers at the end of the first volume of her *Autobiography* (1877): how absurdly unprofessional it is to wait upon inspiration, how necessary to enforce upon oneself regular hours of work, and how everyone seems to start later in the day than she does. Charlotte Brontë once told her how she used to draft a novel into a small notebook, and then copy it all out carefully for the printer; and most authors admitted to her that they found their craft addictive.

The most curious variations, as Harriet Martineau saw herself, relate to the matter of hours. Balzac often wrote frenetically into the night; Dickens during the day; and Trollope and Graham Greene before breakfast. Trollope advocated fast composition or 'hot pressure' for the best work, and his famous account in the *Autobiography* tells how he had himself called daily at 5 a.m. with a pot of coffee, to write 2500 words before going to work. The account provoked J. B. Priestley, in a new edition of the book in 1962, to confess that he often worked best when tired, 'probably because at such times the creative unconscious more readily comes to his aid'. Zola, whose motto was 'Not a day without a line', wrote every morning from 10 a.m. to 1 p.m., covering four or five quarto sheets, and starting with drafts and character sketches which he later documented factually as he worked towards a chapter plan. Raymond Chandler used to say he never forced himself, but kept several hours of the day when he either wrote or did nothing; and Joyce Cary would make a rough synopsis and write whatever part of his projected novel he felt himself able to write, wherever it came.

Some novelists, like Henry James, have shifted from writing to dictation, with some accompanying tendency to prolixity. But it seems clear that most novelists write and rewrite themselves, whether with pen or typewriter. They are manual workers; conscious, and even proud, of the physical labour involved. And most living novelists seem surprised when asked whether they write their chapters in the order they are to appear in, as if unaware there could be any other way: Cary's habit must be exceptional. It seems likely that the commonest way down the centuries to write a novel is as most readers imagine, if they think about the question at all: from start to finish, and from no more notes or forethought than a simple outline, whether on the page or in the head; many novelists being content to revise on the page and in a single process, and leave it at that.

PLANNING AND REVISION

A novel most commonly moves through four stages: from the original idea or germ, through a gestatory period of reflection, and on to composition and then revision. But compared with other literary forms, it has often been a careless art, and one wide in its tolerances. Maupassant used to advise young authors to 'get black on white' or draft quickly, though he also believed in revision. Not everyone has. In his memoir of Smollett (1821), Scott tells how *Sir Lancelot Greaves* (1762) was dashed off by Smollett in monthly instalments:

> When post-time drew near, he used to retire for half an hour or an hour to prepare the necessary quantity of *copy*, as it is technically called in the printing-house, which he never gave himself the trouble to correct, or even to read over,

with the result that the novel includes a number of carelessly inconsistent details. The case may not be exceptional. The sheer scale of many novels in the eighteenth and nineteenth centuries, and the speed at which they were often composed, make it likely enough to have been ordinary. And the twentieth century is not always more deliberate: Angus Wilson has claimed to have written *Anglo-Saxon Attitudes* (1956) in four months, though it is an extensive novel,[1] and Hugh Walpole even worried about his own facility. 'I don't revise much', he once told an interviewer:

In fact I don't revise at all. It goes down, and there it stays. Galsworthy showed me a manuscript of his that was just black. . . . I went home and scratched out masses of sentences, and rewrote them no better than they were before. Then I gave it up. . . .[2]

On the other hand, intensive revision does occur: Trollope, whose effects seldom strike the reader as carefully deliberated or highly polished, claims in his *Autobiography* to have read everything through at least four times – three in manuscript and once in proof; his surviving manuscripts show abundant revision; and Hemingway once said he wrote and rewrote the last page of *Farewell to Arms* (1929) thirty-nine times. But it reads as laconically as the rest – a hero's farewell to his dead mistress in a hospital room:

> But after I had got them out and shut the door and turned off the light it wasn't any good. It was like saying good-bye to a statue. After a while I went out and left the hospital and walked back to the hotel in the rain.

Scott was always notorious for rapid composition, even before debt chained him to his desk. His son-in-law Lockhart, in his *Life* (1837–8), tells how in 1814 a neighbour had watched from across an Edinburgh street as his hand moved ceaselessly across the pages, hour upon hour, to write *Waverley*:

> Page after page is finished and thrown on that heap of MS., and still it goes on unwearied – and so it will be till candles are brought in, and God knows how long after that. It is the same every night. . . . (ch. 7)

Scott's surviving manuscripts are legible, for all that, though haste often caused him to run words together, and he economically sets his lines close on the page and allows himself only the narrowest of margins. (Such economies are not merely Scottish; Trollope once wrote to a friend: 'I utterly repudiate the printers' rule of writing only on one side of my paper.') As for revision, there are occasional deletions in the Waverley novels, but the most striking evidence they offer lies in Scott's fondness for additions, largely made as afterthoughts on the back of the preceding sheet which – unlike Trollope – he had usually left blank at the first drafting; their place in the main text being marked by a caret-sign or inverted 'v'. Such additions can number three or four to a page, and are usually brief, though some are dozens of words long, even half a page. His mottoes were often written in at once, to all appearances, and not as afterthoughts.

Where Scott enlarges, Jane Austen corrects. The two rejected chapters of *Persuasion* show considerable erasure and alteration on the page. But she cared little for textual accidentals such as punctuation, though much for her choice of words, and often uses abbreviations (especially for the names of characters), as if content to leave such matters to the printers – along with a superabundance of dashes that beg to be omitted.

Flaubert revised and rewrote intensively, refining and reducing his drafts to a tiny distillation of his first attempt. But he is pre-eminently the self-conscious artist among novelists of his age. Though the great Victorians such as Dickens and Trollope correct, delete and add on the page, sometimes extensively, their surviving manuscripts often suggest that a single version was enough for them, with revisions made on the manuscript itself; so that many of their stylistic triumphs were presumably gained by the sheer fervour of writing regularly, and at high speed. James was fond of emphasising the contrast between the deliberate artistry of French novelists of his younger days and the culpably relaxed view of the English in such matters: and if the contrast is between Flaubert and Trollope, both of whom he knew personally, he may have been right. But that contrast no longer looked so sharp by the end of the century, with James himself at work, as well as Conrad and Ford; and in the early twentieth, D. H. Lawrence could write draft after draft of the same chapter – once claiming, in a letter of March 1914, to have begun *Women in Love* (1920) 'for about the eleventh time'. Rewriting is a third possibility here, and distinct equally from revising little and revising much. With Proust the case is different again: the afterthought has triumphed, and manuscripts of *A la recherche* show enormous balloons that threaten to swamp the first draft.

It is an open question how much novelists usually prepare before they write. An outline or scenario, whether on the page or in the head, sounds like an elementary precaution, and must always have been common. The reshaped ending of *Persuasion* suggests that Jane Austen, whose effects strike one as exceptionally deliberated, was capable of changing her mind about how a story should best be executed, even when the story itself remains essentially unchanged.

Where does creation begin? Many novels must have been built around a climactic scene that was imagined first; some such scenes are conclusions, and pull the novelist onwards and through. In his 1832 introduction to *Fleetwood*, William Godwin tells how he 'invented' the third and last volume of *Caleb Williams* (1794) first, or conceived the story for it, working backwards in his mind to the start; though he may still have composed the novel from beginning to end. William Golding, in a similar way, once remarked that *The Lord of the Flies* (1954) began in his mind with the last page, where a naval officer rescues a terrified boy from his pursuers. And E. M. Forster has told how, when he began *A Passage to India* (1924), he knew that 'something important happened in the Malabar Caves', though he did not know what it would be.[3]

The first glimpse, however, need not always be of the crux of the story itself. Turgenev claimed to be possessed by images or mental pictures of a character before the story formed in his mind, but he remarked of *Rudin* (1856), his first novel, that he had first conceived of a secondary character there, and of Rudin himself only through him.

Taking notes seems to be a Victorian and twentieth-century characteristic: the great naturalists, like Zola, were famous for it, as in the documentation of coal-mining required to write *Germinal* (1885). But earlier than that, and less pretentiously, Dickens could write 'mems' or memoranda to himself; the manuscript of *Great Expectations* (1860) at Wisbech includes lists of dates establishing the events of the novel, with the ages of characters and hours of the tide – none of it meant to be printed. Barbara Pym has talked recently of how she started writing novels in the 1950s by scribbling down in little notebooks things she had seen and thought of; she later 'boiled it all up and reduced it, like making chutney' (*The Times* [14 September 1977]). But that is observation, not research. Thomas Hardy, who was anxiously aware of his lack of formal education, kept a commonplace book and copied passages from his reading, to be used as he wrote; and George Eliot's habit of research, which was natural to so scholarly a mind, grew on her in later life, when she depended less on recollection and more on published sources. Thackeray took notes for his three historical novels, *Henry Esmond, The Virginians* and *Denis Duval*, mainly based on his eighteenth-century reading, and at his death in 1863 more than a quarter of his library was found to belong to that century; a five-page notebook representing the first third of *Henry Esmond* survives in the New York Public Library. And Joyce seems to have collected phrases for *Ulysses*, as if he were writing a poem rather than a novel, underlining them in various crayons, each colour representing an episode.

Revision can be aesthetic or prudential. Aesthetic revision is a surprisingly minor element, so far as the surviving evidence permits one to say: surprising when one considers how hasty the first composition of many great novels must have been. But it is a convention of fiction, that sprawling art, that even mistakes should often be allowed to stand. Lesage, exceptionally for a novelist in his century, rewrote much of his first novel, *Le Diable boiteux* (1707), for the edition of 1726, redoubling his attack on the Inquisition; Prévost modernised the grammar of *Manon Lescaut* (1731) for a new edition of 1753; and Maria Edgeworth, who by and large altered little, recalls in her letter of 1834 how she removed two witticisms from the first edition of *The Absentee* (1812) as being inconsistent with the character of a speaker; and she sometimes altered details to distinguish a character from his original in life, to cover her tracks. Balzac was notorious for correcting and even rewriting in proof, a habit that eroded his literary profits; and Henry James often revised his novels in a minor sense for their earlier editions following the first, and massively rewrote most of them in his sixties for the New York edition of 1907–9 – *Roderick Hudson*, *The American* and *The Portrait of a Lady*, all early novels, being reworked the most intensively. The manuscript of D. H. Lawrence's *Sons and Lovers* (1913) in the University of California at Berkeley has numerous cuts made by his publisher, Edward Garnett – not, as one might expect, in the way of censorship, but merely to prune a repetitious style. They are much to be welcomed.

But it remains exceptional for a novelist to possess both the will and the opportunity to revise a novel on aesthetic grounds after it has been published. It can even smack of self-importance: it certainly calls for self-justification. When John Fowles revised *The Magus* (1966) in 1977, he subtitled it *A Revised Version* for an age in which both subtitles and revisions are exceptional in novels, and added a defensive foreword that justified stylistic revision on the grounds that it was essentially the first written of his books.

Prudential revision can be more imperative. When Disraeli's novels were collected in 1853, he had by that time been Chancellor of the Exchequer; and he pruned the earliest of them, such as *Vivian Grey* (1826), of what had come over the years to look vulgar or potentially libellous, cutting scenes and even whole chapters. The Coningsby trilogy, however, which was written after he had entered the Commons in 1837, was left essentially unaltered. Hardy could revise in a reverse sense, as in *Jude the Obscure* (1896), where he restored some expurgations made for the severer world of serial publication; though he could still vacillate, altering 'sex' to 'affection' and back to 'sex' again; and he continued to tamper with the texts of his collected editions even after he had ceased writing novels. And the Texas manuscript of Lawrence's *Women in Love* includes two early chapters omitted from the book, the first evidently suppressed for fear of sexual offence.

But such cases remain unusual. Some novelists lose interest when the manuscript has gone to the printer. Some cannot proofread, even if they would. Some, like F. Scott Fitzgerald, never even learn to spell. Many are willing to leave the tedious business of correction to a publisher's reader, or to posterity.

The novel, as a result, is a mighty task for an army of editors. And yet it is the least edited of all the literary kinds, at least in English, even though none, paradoxically, leaves so much for the scholar to do. That it remains under-edited to this day is perhaps a survival of what was once its universal lack of status – a lack that lingers on vestigially in academies. Some institutional libraries, even now, decline to catalogue novels, and especially new novels, along with other books.

MANUSCRIPTS

Autographs, or manuscripts from the hand of the author himself, survive only rarely for eighteenth-century novels, and it is doubtful if anyone took much interest in such objects before the rage for collecting in the present century. The manuscripts of early novels would commonly be thrown away by the printer rather than returned to the author.

Among institutional libraries, it is doubtful if any has interested itself in such manuscripts before the present century. The D. H. Lawrence collection at the University of Texas, the Thomas Mann collection in the University of Zurich, and the Virginia Woolf collection in the University of Sussex, all suggest that the tide of fashion has at last turned towards these materials as objects of study – but only since the Second World War. As for individuals, Hugh Walpole was perhaps the first novelist, and even the first person, to collect autographs of novels, which he began to acquire in 1918 out of a passion for Scott. His collection, along with much of Somerset Maugham's, is now in their old school, King's at Canterbury. But it is only within memory that autographs like these have become cult-objects: a turning-point, perhaps, was E. M. Forster's gift of his autograph of *A Passage to India* in 1960, to save the London Library, when it was sold to America for £6,500 – a price then unexampled for a manuscript by a living author.

The subject remains essentially unexplored. There is still no comprehensive survey of fictional manuscripts and their locations, though studies of individual novelists based on their papers are fast increasing. This chapter offers an introductory outline.

The eighteenth century, and still more the seventeenth, are almost blanks. No autograph of a novel, or of any part of one, survives from the hand of Defoe, Richardson or Smollett; or of Lesage, Marivaux or Crébillon *fils*. The earliest survivor seems to be seventeenth-century German, in the early drafts and revisions of Duke Anton Ulrich von Braunschweig's *Octavia*, a vast historical romance on the Rome of the early Christians that began to appear in 1677, and on which the noble author worked for nearly forty years. The manuscripts are at Wolfenbüttel, near Brunswick, and probably represent the earliest surviving autograph of a novel by any known author.

After 1700 the field is only slightly richer. There are autographs of Voltaire's *contes*, and Sterne's *Sentimental Journey* survives in the British Library in London: a lightly corrected fair copy, though incomplete, in a clear italic hand, and probably the first English novel to survive in the hand of its author. An accompanying letter from its owner in 1843 tells how his grandfather had 'valued it highly', receiving it from a friend of Sterne himself. Its French equivalent among novels may be Rousseau's *La Nouvelle Héloïse*, of which manuscripts and drafts survive in Paris, Geneva and elsewhere, including copies made by Rousseau for friends. These two cases, essentially simultaneous, suggest that by the 1760s a friend of a novelist might esteem his autograph as a memento of their acquaintance.

For the nineteenth century, the survival is more abundant. None of Jane Austen's six novels remain, apart from two rejected chapters of *Persuasion* in the British Library; but her three volumes of juvenilia, mainly burlesque and composed in 1787–93, between her twelfth year and her eighteenth, have survived in fair copies which she was probably made to read aloud from to her family circle; and he autograph of her unfinished novel *Sanditon*, abandoned in March 1817 just before her death, is now in King's College, Cambridge.

Scott is the first novelist in English to survive considerably in autographs of his major works. Many are in the Pierpont Morgan Library in New York, including *Guy Mannering, The Antiquary, Old Mortality, Ivanhoe, Peveril of the Peak, Quentin Durward* and others; while the National Library of Scotland in Edinburgh has *The Heart of Midlothian* and *Redgauntlet,* with *Kenilworth* in the British Library and *The Fortunes of Nigel* at King's School, Canterbury – a manuscript that belonged to Ruskin before it came to Hugh Walpole. Most of these autographs were not used by the printers, who were given transcripts made to preserve Scott's anonymity, and their survival is the less surprising for that reason. They were given by Scott to his publisher for concealment, and were auctioned by the publisher's creditors in Edinburgh just before his death, in 1831, for disappointingly small sums.

The Victorian landscape is richly stocked. Charlotte Brontë's fair copy of *Jane Eyre,* made in 1847, is in the British Library, and much of Dickens is in the Forster collection in the Victoria and Albert Museum, though *Great Expectations* was presented to Wisbech Museum, along with the autograph of M. G. Lewis's *Monk.* Balzac and Flaubert have survived massively, and have been edited more attentively than their English contemporaries. Trollope's autographs, essentially unused by editors, are almost all in the USA, the only novel to remain in England being *Framley Parsonage,* which (lacking its first eighteen chapters) has been given to his old school at Harrow. Of Henry James's twenty and more novels, only two survive complete as autographs, along with notebooks and many letters: *The Princess Casamassima* and *Confidence* are at Harvard, as well as his study of Trollope, while a part of *The Other House* is in the Walpole collection in Canterbury; Harvard also has the printed pages of *The American* and of *The Portrait of a Lady* extensively revised by James in the margins for the New York edition of 1907–9.

Joyce, being the centre of an international circle, seems to have attracted collectors early: perhaps earlier than any other European novelist. The *Ulysses* autograph was sold against Joyce's wishes by one collector to another as early as 1924, or only two years after its publication, and it remains in private hands, though it is by now one of the few novels to have been published in facsimile as a manuscript. An early version of his *Portrait of the Artist,* written in 1903, was acquired by Harvard and published as *Stephen Hero* in 1944; the final manuscript of the novel being in the National Library of Ireland in

Dublin. Most of *Finnegans Wake* is in the British Library.

★

So scattered a record suggests a study in its early stage: its materials only recently valued or thought worth preserving, its documents still largely unedited in a modern sense, its status still unclear in the world of thought. If in future times this book could be seen as a primitive sketch long since surpassed by historians of wider range and deeper perception, it will have satisfied an ambition and fulfilled a purpose.

NOTES

1. *Writers at Work*, edited by Malcolm Cowley (London, 1958) p. 229.
2. *Everyman* 4 June 1931.
3. *Writers at Work*, p. 26.

Notes for Further Reading

These notes relate to chapters of the book, omitting chapters 9 and 10, and beginning with works of reference. The place of publication is given, unless it is London, following the short title.

★

There is an international guide with extensive German plot-summaries in *Der Romanführer*, edited by Wilhelm Olbrich *et al.*, revised in 15 vols (Stuttgart: 1960–71).

For English catalogues see C. C. Mish, *English Prose Fiction 1600–1700* (Charlottesville: 1952, revised 1967); W. H. McBurney, *A Check List of English Prose Fiction 1700–39* (Cambridge, Mass.: 1960); Andrew Block, *The English Novel 1740–1850* (1939, revised 1961). There is a symposium on secondary material in *Victorian Fiction*, edited by Lionel Stevenson (Cambridge, Mass.: 1964).

For French catalogues see Maurice Lever, *La Fiction narrative en prose au XVIIème siècle* (Paris: 1976); Silas P. Jones, *A List of French Prose Fiction from 1700 to 1750* (New York: 1939); Angus Martin, V. G. Mylne and Richard Frautschi, *Bibliographie du genre romanesque français 1751–1800* (1977).

There are critical anthologies in *Novelists on the Novel*, edited by Miriam Allott (1959) and Henri Coulet, *Le Roman jusqu'à la Révolution* (Paris: 1968). William Freeman, *Dictionary of Fictional Characters* (1963, revised and indexed as *Everyman's Dictionary*, 1973) is based on novels, etc. in English only.

I AN APOLOGY FOR FICTION

Criticism of the novel is not an invention of the 1960s, though that age saw a revival in theories of narrative. See, for instance, Daniel Huet, *Traité de l'origine des romans* (Paris: 1670, edited by A. Kok, Amsterdam: 1942); Mme de Staël, *Essai sur les fictions* (Lausanne: 1795), on the moral power of realism, a work promptly translated by Goethe; Clara Reeve, *The Progress of Romance* (1785); Anna Barbauld, 'On the Origins and Progress of Novel-Writing', in *British Novelists* vol. I (1810); Flaubert's letters from the 1840s till his death in 1880, which began to appear in 1884, now edited by Jean Bruneau (Paris: 1973–) and selected as *Extraits*, edited by G. Bollème (Paris: 1963); David Masson, *British Novelists and Their Styles* (1859); R. H. Hutton's Victorian reviews, some reprinted in Critical Heritage volumes; and Henry James, *Notebooks*, edited by F. O. Matthiessen and Kenneth Murdock (New York: 1955), which he kept 1878–1900 – still the finest compendium of the creative act.

For recent debates, the first volume of the American periodical *Novel* in 1967 includes articles by Ian Watt, Wayne C. Booth, Frank Kermode and David Lodge, defending earlier positions; and *Europe* (Paris) collects the views of some fifty novelists as 'Le roman par les romanciers' (October 1968). Iris Murdoch has spoken eloquently for social realism in 'The Sublime and Beautiful Revisited', *Yale Review* 49 (1959) and in 'Against Dryness', *Encounter* (Jan. 1961), the latter reprinted in *The Novel Today*, edited by Malcolm Bradbury (1977); the argument is continued in J. P. Stern, *On Realism* (1973).

For the opposing case, see *Tel quel* (Paris: 1962) for the views of Nathalie Sarraute, Michel Butor, A. Robbe-Grillet and others; R. Scholes and R. Kellogg, *The Nature of Narrative* (New York: 1966); Roland Bourneuf and Réal Ouellet, *L'Univers du roman* (Paris: 1972); two lectures by Frank Kermode, *Novel and Narrative* (Glasgow: 1972) and *How We Read Novels* (Southampton: 1975); David Lodge, *The Modes of Modern Writing* (1977); and for a temperate view of the controversy, Bernard Bergonzi, *The Situation of the Novel* (1970, with new preface 1972).

2   MEMOIRS

René Démoris, *Le roman à la première personne* (Paris: 1975) starts with the seventeenth century; Bertil Romberg, *Studies in the Narrative Technique of the First-Person Novel* (Stockholm: 1962) is mainly based on modern instances. See also V. G. Mylne, *The Eighteenth-Century French Novel* (Manchester: 1965) ch. 3; Philip Stewart, *Imitation and Illusion in the French Memoir-Novel 1700–50* (New Haven: 1969); and English Showalter, *The Evolution of the French Novel 1641–1782* (Princeton: 1972). On narrative points of view, see Wayne C. Booth, *The Rhetoric of Fiction* (Chicago: 1961) and Norbert Miller, *Der empfindsame Erzähler* (Munich: 1968).

On the picaresque, see Claudio Guillén, 'Toward a Definition of the Picaresque' (1961), in his *Literature as System* (Princeton: 1971) and A. A. Parker, *Literature and the Delinquent* (Edinburgh: 1967); on the cervantic, E. C. Riley, *Cervantes's Theory of the Novel* (Oxford: 1962); and on stream of consciousness, Edouard Dujardin, *Le Monologue intérieur* (Paris: 1931), M. J. Friedman, *Stream of Consciousness* (1955); Leon Edel, *The Psychological Novel 1900–50* (1955); and Robert Humphrey, *Stream of Consciousness in the Modern Novel* (Berkeley: 1959).

3 LETTERS

Natascha Würzbach, *The Novel in Letters* (1969), on English fiction 1678–1740, first appeared in German in 1964; see also Robert A. Day, *Told in Letters* (Ann Arbor: 1966). For the French, see V. G. Mylne, *The Eighteenth-Century French Novel* (Manchester: 1965) ch. 8, or the earlier C. E. Kany, *The Beginnings of the Epistolary Novel* (Berkeley: 1937).

4 DIALOGUE

Dialogue is much discussed by Flaubert in his letters (see 1, above), especially the problems of common speech. For English see Norman Page, *Speech in the English Novel* (1973). There is a full study of *style indirect libre* in Roy Pascal, *The Dual Voice* (Manchester: 1977), and of the relation of dialogue with other modes in Graham Hough, 'Narrative and Dialogue in Jane Austen' (1970) in his *Selected Essays* (Cambridge: 1978).

See also V. G. Mylne, in J. H. Fox (ed.) 'Dialogue as Narrative in Eighteenth-Century Fiction', in *Studies in Eighteenth-Century Literature Presented to Robert Niklaus* (Exeter: 1975); and Patricia Ingham, 'Dialect in the Novels of Hardy and George Eliot', in George Watson (ed.) *Literary English since Shakespeare* (New York: 1970).

5 TITLES AND DEVICES

On anonymity see S. Halkett and J. Laing, *A Dictionary of the Anonymous and Pseudonymous Literature of Gt Britain*, 4 vols (1882–8, revised 1926–34 with supplements), and A. A. Barbier, *Dictionnaire des ouvrages anonymes*, 4 vols (revised Paris: 1882). See also Ian Watt, 'The Naming of Characters in Defoe, Richardson and Fielding',

Review of English Studies XXV (1949); and Philip Stevick, *The Chapter in Fiction* (Syracuse NY: 1970).

6   BEGINNING AND ENDING

Maurice Lever, *La Fiction narrative en prose au XVIIème siècle* (Paris: 1976) quotes opening sentences. See *Romananfänge*, edited by Norbert Miller (Berlin: 1965), a collection of essays on endings as well as beginnings; Frank Kermode, *The Sense of an Ending* (1967); and Edward W. Said, *Beginnings* (New York: 1975).

7   TENSE AND TIME

An early work on the grammar of fiction was Franz K. Stanzel, *Narrative Situations in the Novel* (Bloomington: 1971), which first appeared in German in 1955; see also his *Grammatik der Erzählkunst* (Göttingen: 1979). There is a general study by A. A. Mendilow, *Time and the Novel* (1952); an account of Sterne's views in J. J. Mayoux, 'Variations in Time and Sense in *Tristram Shandy*', in A. H. Cash and J. M. Stedmond (eds), *The Winged Skull* (1971); and of Proust's in Gérard Genette, 'Time and Narrative in *A la recherche du temps perdu*', in J. H. Miller (ed.) *Aspects of Narrative* (New York: 1971) and, more extensively, in his *Figures III* (Paris: 1972). See also G. Müller, 'Erzählzeit und erzählte Zeit', in his *Morphologische Poetik* (Tübingen: 1968).

On tense see Harald Weinrich, *Tempus: besprochene und erzählte Welt* (Stuttgart: 1964, revised 1971) and C. P. Casparis, *Tense without Time* (Berne: 1975). There is an earlier account in Käthe Hamburger, *Die Logik der Dichtung* (Stuttgart: 1957, revised 1968) discussed by Roy Pascal in 'Tense and Novel', *Modern Language Review* LVII (1962).

8   HISTORY IN ITS PLACE

Ernest A. Baker, *A Guide to Historical Fiction* (1914) lists novels by the periods they describe, from prehistory to the early twentieth century; see also D. D. McGarry and S. H. White, *Historical Fiction Guide* (New York: 1963). Georg Lukács, *Der historische Roman* (Moscow: 1937) was not translated into English till 1962; on the problems of the modern novelist see Mary Renault, 'History in Fiction', *Times Literary Supplement* (23 March 1973); and on Scott's influence, G. M. Trevelyan, *An Autobiography* (1949). Donald Davie, *The Heyday of Scott* (1961) considers his international influence; see also Marilyn Butler, *Maria Edgeworth* (Oxford: 1972), especially ch. 8. On regionalism, Phyllis

Bentley, *The English Regional Novel* (1941); L. Leclaire, *Le Roman régionaliste dans les Iles Britanniques 1800–1950* (Paris: 1954).

11   HOW NOVELISTS WRITE

There is no catalogue of novel-manuscripts; but numerous studies exist of the genesis of individual works, notably in the introductions to the Garnier editions of classic French fiction. For more extended studies see Giles R. Hoyt, *The Development of Anton Ulrich's Narrative Prose on the Basis of Surviving Octavia Manuscripts and Prints* (Bonn: 1977); Hermine de Saussure, *Etude sur le sort des manuscrits de J.-J. Rousseau* (Neuchâtel: 1974); B. C. Southam, *Jane Austen's Literary Manuscripts* (Oxford: 1964); and R. F. Christian, *Tolstoy's War and Peace* (Oxford: 1962); and Philip Gaskell, *From Writer to Reader* (Oxford, 1978) on Richardson and Joyce.

On Flaubert's early attempts, Jean Bruneau, *Les Débuts littéraires de Flaubert* (Paris: 1962), and Claudine Gothot-Mersch, *La Genèse de Madame Bovary* (Paris: 1966); and on Zola, H. Massis, *Comment Zola composait ses romans* (Paris: 1906). Proust's processes have been extensively studied in Albert Feuillerat, *Comment Proust a composé son roman* (New Haven: 1934) and in Alison Winton, *Proust's Additions*, 2 vols (Cambridge: 1977),

Letters apart, there are records by novelists themselves, such as André Gide's *Journal des Faux-monnayeurs* (Paris: 1926); Thomas Wolfe, *The Story of a Novel* (1936), on writing *Of Time and the River* (1935); and Thomas Mann, *Die Entstehung des Doktor Faustus: Roman eines Romans* (Amsterdam: 1949). And there are numerous published interviews, notably in the *Paris Review*, collected as *Writers at Work*, edited by Malcolm Cowley *et al.* (New York: 1958–).

Facsimiles are now becoming available, such as Jane Austen's unfinished *Sanditon*, edited by B. C. Southam (Oxford: 1975) and Henry James's revision of his published novel *The American* of 1877 for the New York edition of 1907, edited by R. G. Dennis (Ilkley: 1976). Others are limited to a page or two, as in the edition of Sterne's *Sentimental Journey* by G. D. Stout (Berkeley: 1967).

Glossary of European Terms

This list is based alphabetically on English terms, where they exist, with certain synonyms and analogues of interest in French, German, Italian and Spanish; and references. For German terms see 'Register der Roman-Arten', in *Der Romanführer* vol. XV, edited by W. Olbrich (1971) pp. 314–83, with instances.

Fr = French   G = German   It = Italian   Sp = Spanish

anti-novel – an experimental novel claiming to break with narrative tradition, such as Samuel Beckett's or Alain Robbe-Grillet's, though it might be applied to much earlier works such as Sterne's *Tristram Shandy*. Fr *anti-roman* perhaps the origin of the English term, though both are common by 1960s. On the other hand, it is part of the title of the second (1633) edition of Charles Sorel's *Le Berger extravagant* (1627), a comic anti-pastoral romance. G *Anti-Roman*.

Bildungsroman, or *Erziehungsroman*, or *Entwicklungsroman* – a novel tracing the psychological formation or education of the hero, from innocence to experience of the world – a form so German as to be internationally known by these terms. Wieland's *Agathon* (1767) is perhaps the first clear instance, and Goethe's *Wilhelm Meisters Lehrjahre* (1795–6) the most famous. The first term was made current by Dilthey in 1870; the second is perhaps better reserved for novels on the education of children, e.g. Rousseau's *Emile* (1762). Fr *roman de formation*. French and English parallels are often only doubtful, like Dickens's *Copperfield* (1850) or Joyce's *Portrait of the Artist* (1916), which a German might prefer to call a *Künstlerroman*, or novel about an artist. See Jürgen Jacobs, *Wilhelm Meister und seine Brüder* (1972); Martin Swales, *The German Bildungsroman from Wieland to Hesse* (1978).

154

cervantic – a comic formula based on Cervantes's *Don Quixote* (1605–15), with master and servant encountering absurd adventures on their journeys – and one of them, at least, the innocent victim of an illusion, like Quixote's about chivalry. French versions include Sorel (*under* anti-novel, *above*) and Marivaux's *Pharsamon* (1737), written 1712; English include Fielding's *Joseph Andrews* (1742), Charlotte Lennox's *The Female Quixote* (1752) and Dickens's *Pickwick* (1836–7), where Dickens follows Fielding in reversing the formula into a fat master and a thin servant. See chapter 2, above.

detective-story – a fiction, often as long as a novel, based on a mystery (usually a crime) unravelled by detection; or *whodunit*; or to librarians and publishers a *crime-novel*. Fr *roman policier*, G *Kriminalroman* (popularly *Krimi*), It *romanzo poliziesco* (popularly *un giallo*, for its yellow cover, though the Fr convention is black, *série noire*), Sp *novela policíaca*. A nineteenth-century invention, from Wilkie Collins's *The Moonstone* (1868) and Conan Doyle's Sherlock Holmes stories beginning with *A Study in Scarlet* (1887) down to Agatha Christie and Simenon. Dickens's *Bleak House* (1853) includes Mr Inspector Bucket, a professional whose wife is an amateur detective. Granting that the detective needs to stand outside the crime itself, earlier novels of criminal mystery like Godwin's *Caleb Williams* (1794) do not qualify. See Julian Symons, *Bloody Murder* (1972).

frame-story or *frame-narrative* – a story linking a series of stories most commonly told by individual characters, as in *Decameron*. No Fr term? G *Rahmenerzählung*, It *cornice* or *novella portante*, Sp *cuadro narrativo*. For a story so enclosed, G *Binnenerzählung*, Fr *le récit de X* (name of character), for which there is no better English equivalent than *X's story*.

free indirect style – a translation of Fr *style indirect libre*, so named by Swiss linguist Charles Bally in 1912; G *erlebte Rede*; It *stile indiretto libero*. It refers to a passage where the distinctive utterance of a character is embedded in narrative with a change of tense (normally from present to past), 'free' of conjunctions, inverted commas or dashes, and phrases like 'he said'. See S. Ullmann, *Style in the French Novel* (Cambridge: 1957); Roy Pascal, *The Dual Voice* (Manchester: 1977). See chapter 4, above.

Gothic novel – a novel of supernatural horror, often with a medieval setting, flourishing for about half a century from Horace Walpole's *Castle of Otranto* (1764), and parodied in Jane Austen's *Northanger Abbey* (1818). Fr *roman noir* and G *Schauerroman* are less historically bound as terms; but Fr *roman gothique* would refer, like the English, to a period around 1800. The G word might need to be qualified to do so; G *Horrorroman* would refer to a recent work. It *romanzo gotico*. Other terms exist, such as *tale of terror* (Fr *roman terrifiant*), like Mary Shelley's *Frankenstein* (1818), descending into *shocker* and *penny dreadful*. See Montague Summers, *The Gothic Quest* (1938) and *A Gothic Bibliography* (1940).

historical novel – a novel set in an historical period, and often including or alluding to historical personages. Fr *roman historique* (or *nouvelle historique*, if briefer), It *romanzo storico*, G *historischer Roman*, Sp *novela histórica*. An expanding form from Mme de La Fayette's *Princesse de Clèves* (1678) to Scott's *Waverley* (1814) and Thackeray's *Esmond* (1852), as well as Dumas, Hugo, Manzoni, Fontane and Tolstoy. See chapters 7–8, above.

letter-novel, or *epistolary novel* – a novel composed wholly or largely in letters from one or more characters, sometimes interspersed with journal or diary. Fr *roman par lettres, roman épistolaire*, G. *Briefroman*, It *romanzo epistolario*, Sp *novela epistolar*. A principal form in mid- and late eighteenth century, from Richardson's *Pamela* (1740) to Laclos's *Liaisons dangereuses* (1782). See chapter 3, above.

memoir-novel – a novel in the first person wholly or largely composed as autobiography or memoirs, usually by a single character, and sometimes interspersed with journal or diary, like Defoe's *Crusoe* (1719). Fr *mémoires*, or *roman sous forme de mémoires*, or *autobiographie-fiction*, G *fiktive Autobiographie*. A wider concept is represented by *first-person novel*, which need not, like the memoir, tell the greater part of a life; Fr *roman à la première personne*, G *Ich-Roman*, It *romanzo in prima persona*, Sp *novela en primera persona*. The term *autobiographical novel* might better be reserved for novels relating to the author's own life, such as Dickens's *Copperfield*, which is a first-person novel, or Joyce's *Portrait*, which is in the third person; or Mark Rutherford's *Autobiography*, of 1881 which is a novel, in spite of its title. A *pseudo-memoir* refers to a novel that tries to pass as genuine autobiography, like the *Mémoires de d'Artagnan* of 1700 that Dumas thought real; Fr *pseudo-mémoires*, G *fingierte Autobiographie*. See chapter 2 above.

narrated time – the length of time represented; Fr *temps de l'histoire*, G *erzählte Zeit*. Contrasted with *narrative time*, or *reader's time*, the time it takes to read; Fr *temps du récit*, G *Erzählzeit*. In most novels, outside dialogue, they are widely distinct, on the whole; though in Mann's *Buddenbrooks* (1901) they move towards correspondence as the novel proceeds.

narrator – a character who tells the story rather than the novelist himself – though sometimes, as with Proust's 'je', the two may be hard to distinguish. Conrad's Marlow, and Raymond Chandler's Marlowe, are instances. Fr *narrateur*, G *Erzähler*, It *narratore*, Sp *narrador*. If the narrator observes the action and takes part in it little, like the Vieillard in Bernardin's *Paul et Virginie* (1787) or Old Thady in Maria Edgeworth's *Castle Rackrent* (1800), he is an *observer-narrator*; an *observer* only, like Strether in Henry James's *Ambassadors* (1903), if the novel is third-person; or (more ambitiously) a *central intelligence*. See Käte Friedemann, *Die Rolle des Erzählers in der Epik* (1910); Wayne C. Booth, 'The Self-Conscious Narrator in Comic Fiction before *Tristram Shandy*', *PMLA*, LXVII (1952).

naturalism – a concern in fiction with the underlying 'laws' of nature and of history, allegedly scientific, such as Darwin's, Marx's or Comte's. Fr *naturalisme*, G *Naturalismus*, It and Sp *naturalismo*. Early examples are the *Germinie Lacerteux* (1865) of the Goncourts, or Zola, who described himself as a *naturaliste* in his preface to *Thérèse Raquin* (1868); later Galdos, Hardy, Gissing, Hauptmann, Dreiser. A successor to *realism*, below. See Pierre Martino, *Le Naturalisme français 1870–95* (1923, revised 1969); René Dumesnil, *Le Réalisme et le naturalisme* (1955); and ch. 9, above.

nouveau roman – French New Novel from 1950s, anticipated by Nathalie Sarraute, *Tropismes* (1938), and embodied in the title of Robbe-Grillet's *Pour un nouveau roman* (1963); often given to clinical description of things, or *chosisme*, and an emphasis on its own fictionality. See John Sturrock, *The French New Novel* (1969).

novel – a fictional prose narrative of length, usually with a claim to describe the real. Fr *roman*, G *Roman*, It *romanzo*, Sp *novela*. Scott, in an article on *romance* in *Encyclopaedia Britannica* (1824), described the novel as 'fictitious narrative, differing from the Romance, because the events are accommodated to the ordinary train of human events, and the modern state of society.' The distinction with *romance* is not available in French, though it was in the seventeenth century; cf Segrais, *Les Nouvelles françoises* (1656): 'Le roman écrit les choses comme la bienséance le veut et à la manière du poète', whereas the *nouvelle* describes things 'comme d'ordinaire nous les voyons arriver . . .', where *roman* = *romance* and *nouvelle* = *novel*. G *Roman* too signifies *romance* as well as *novel*; a medieval verse romance, however, can be distinguished as *höfisches Epos*. An English instance of *novel*, arguably in its modern sense, has been found earlier than Milton's, or in 1639; see J. J. O'Connor, *Notes & Queries* November 1953.

novelette – once a short novel, now one of slight value, often romantic in theme. Fr *novelette*, G *Unterhaltungsroman* (if merely entertaining), It *romanzetto*, Sp *novelita*.

Novelle, *nouvelle* – see **tale**, below.

picaresque – Sp *pícaro* means a wily rogue, and the form arises in sixteenth-century Spain, involving the cunning servant of a succession of masters. G *Schelmenroman* (also adjectives *pikaresk* or *pikarisch*, like Fr *picaresque*, It and Sp *picaresco*). See chapter 2, above.

plot – outline or plan of a story; now more often the story itself. Fr *histoire*, *intrigue*, *action*, G *Handlung*, *Fabel*, It and Sp *trama*; many of these terms from dramatic criticism.

realism – a down-to-earth, even brutal, account of modern reality, claiming to fidelity; so used as a literary term in Fr, *réalisme*, since 1820s, and flourishing as a school of fiction since mid-nineteenth century. G *Realismus*, It and Sp *realismo*, or *verismo*, which can suggest something more detailed and minute. Often qualified by *social*, *psychological*, *poetic*, etc. See E. B. O. Borgerhoff, *'Réalisme* and kindred words', *PMLA*, LIII (1938); 'Realism, Reality and the Novel', *Novel*, II (1969).

regional novel – a novel representing the life of a region. Fr *roman régionaliste*, It *romanzo regionale*, G *Heimatroman*, Sp *novela regional* (or *novela costumbrista*, on local customs). From Rousseau and Maria Edgeworth, through Brontës, George Sand, Keller, Hardy, Verga. See L. Leclaire, *A General Bibliography of the Regional Novelists of the British Isles 1800–1950* (1954), and chapter 8, above.

roman à clef – a novel including real characters under fictitious names, to be guessed by some. G *Schlüsselroman*, It *romanzo a chiave*, Sp *novela de clave*. Keys could be provided, at least in some editions; or published separately. Disraeli's *Coningsby* (1844) provoked two anonymous keys (1844), not by him; and Harriet Beecher Stowe followed her *Uncle Tom's Cabin* (1851) with her own *Key*, 'verifying the truth of the work', though through types rather than individuals.

roman à thèse – a thesis or propaganda novel, often in the cause of political or religious change. G *Tendenzroman*, Sp *novela de tesis*. Examples are Diderot's *Religieuse*, which is anti-monastic, Disraeli's *Sybil* on Tory radicalism, and much of Zola, Galsworthy and Upton Sinclair.

saga – a series of novels often about a family, like Mann's *Joseph und seine Brüder* (1933–44). Fr *roman fleuve*, a term coined by Romain Rolland and commonly used in other languages, as for his *Jean-Christophe* (1904–12); G *Romanzyklus*. Galsworthy used *saga* for the Forsytes; Balzac, who develops the notion of *le retour des personnages*, is perhaps its first master. Proust's *A la recherche* qualifies to the extent that characters age and return. But that recurrence, though necessary, is not sufficient, as P. G. Wodehouse's ageless Jeeves and Wooster prove. There are recent instances by C. P. Snow, Anthony Powell and Doris Lessing. See Elizabeth M. Kerr, *Bibliography of the Sequence Novel* (1950); A. R. Pugh, *Balzac's Recurring Characters* (1974), and Angela Bianchini, *Il romanzo d'appendice* (Turin: 1969).

science-fiction, or *SF* – novels set in a technically advanced future. Fr *science-fiction* or *littérature d'anticipation*, G *Zukunftsroman*, It *fanta-scienza*, Sp *ciencia-ficción*. But *SF* is internationally understood. Though by now highly Anglo-American, its chief pioneer, Jules Verne, was French of the 1860s, followed by H. G. Wells in 1890s. See Joseph H. Crawford, *333: A Bibliography of the Science-Fantasy Novel*

(1953); Kingsley Amis, *New Maps of Hell* (1967); Pierre Versins, *Encyclopedie* (Lausanne, 1972).

serial – a novel published in parts – whether independent parts, as in Dickens, or in a periodical, in which case Fr *roman-feuilleton*, such as Dumas's *Trois Mousquetaires* (1844). G *Fortsetzungsroman*, It *romanzo a puntate* or *romanzo d'appendice* (now usually derogatory).

stream of consciousness – the unspoken thoughts of a character used as a radical device of narrative. Fr *monologue intérieur*, G *innerer Monolog*, *Bewusstseinsstrom*, It *monologo interiore*, *flusso di conscienza*, Sp *monólogo interior*. The English term, coined by William James in *Principles of Psychology* (1890), is familiar in much foreign critical prose. Pioneered by Edouard Dujardin in *Les Lauriers sont coupés* (1888) and developed by Joyce, Proust, Dorothy Richardson, Hermann Broch, Virginia Woolf and Faulkner. See chapter 2, above.

tale – imprecise in English, but most specifically a short novel, usually with a single strand of narrative – though it can also mean a short story. G *Novelle*, a short novel, is highly specific; see Martin Swales, *The German Novelle* (1977). Fr *nouvelle* or *conte*, It *romanzo breve* (*novella* and *racconto* = short story), Sp *cuento*, which can also mean a short story, as Sp *novela corte* can = Fr *nouvelle*. Fr *nouvelle* and *conte* are commonly less realistic than the *roman*, and in the third person; see René Godenne, *La Nouvelle française* (1974); whereas G *Novelle* from the early nineteenth century was often felt to be more realistic than the *Roman*, if only ironically so. Fr *conte philosophique* is a short novel of ideas, like Voltaire's *Candide*; *conte moral* is an edifying one, like Johnson's *Rasselas* – but Fr *moral* can refer to *moeurs* or manners as well as to morality, and means both in Marmontel's *Contes moraux* (1761). English novels fit the notion of *conte* only imprecisely: Peacock's novels, Butler's *Erewhon*, Waugh's *Decline and Fall*, Orwell's *Animal Farm*.

thriller – a novel of exciting and sensational events, but realistic to the extent of excluding the supernatural or the gothic. Fr *roman policier*, *roman d'aventures*, *roman d'espionage*; G *Abenteuerroman*, *Thriller* (or popularly *Reisser*); It *romanzo di suspense*; Sp *novela de suspenso*. From Poe in 1840s, when he avoids the supernatural, to Anthony Hope, John Buchan and Ian Fleming. Many cases overlap with *detective-story*, above.

Index